KU-713-644

A Primary Teacher's Handbook Design and Technology

Georgina Stein
Philip Poole

Acknowledgements

Folens allows photocopying of pages marked 'copiable page' for educational use, providing that this use is within the confines of the purchasing institution. Copiable pages should not be declared in any return in respect of any photocopying licence.

Folens books are protected by international copyright laws. All rights are reserved. The copyright of all materials in this book, except where otherwise stated, remains the property of the publisher and author(s). No part of this publication may be reproduced, stored in a retrieval system, or transmitted, in any form or by any means, for whatever purpose, without the written permission of Folens Limited.

Georgina Stein (Roehampton Institute London) and Philip Poole (Canterbury Christ Church College) hereby assert their moral rights to be identified as the authors of this work in accordance with the Copyright, Designs and Patents Act 1988.

Material to support planning schemes of work are reproduced by permission of Lewisham Professional Development Centre.

Editor: Claire Ancell
Design: Andy Bailey
Layout artist: Patricia Hollingsworth
Cover image: Georgina Stein and Ray Young
Cover design: Kim Ashby and John Hawkins

© 1997 Folens Limited, on behalf of the authors.
Every effort has been made to contact copyright holders of material used in this book. If any have been overlooked, we will be pleased to make any necessary arrangements.

First published 1997 by Folens Limited, Dunstable and Dublin. Folens Limited, Albert House, Apex Business Centre, Boscombe Road, Dunstable, LU5 4RL, England.

The authors and publisher would like to thank the following:

Peter Codling, Raynes Park High School, London Borough of Merton; Mrs E Collison Rainhill and Rev E Collison, Rainhill, Prescot, Merseyside; Lesley Brooks, Woodley, Berkshire; Angela Cook, staff and pupils at Broomwood Hall; Andrea Stephens and Sandra Hall, Radstock County Primary School, Berkshire County Council; BA (QTS) students, Roehampton Institute London; Technology Teaching Systems (TTS), Monk Road, Alfreton (Tel: 01773 830255 Fax: 01773 830325); LEGO Dacta, the educational division of the LEGO Group, for permission to show LEGO model on page 36.

And the staff and pupils of:
The Bulmershe School, Colleton Primary School, Radstock County Primary School, Waingels Copse School, Willow Bank County Junior School.

With thanks also to:
Tony Turner for his work on product evaluation.
Rev Ian Hartland
Andrew Lofts and Tristram Shepard for their disassembly ideas.
Lewisham Primary Teachers and Hind Makia who developed the curriculum planning tools.

Photographs:
Georgina Stein and Ray Young – pages 15, 21, 22, 23, 24 (top), 25, 26, 29, 30, 38, 39, 45 (bottom), 48, 53, 58
Georgina Stein – pages 31 (bottom), 34, 47, 52
LEGO UK – page 36
Technology Teaching Systems – pages, 4, 7, 9, 24, 27, 28, 33, 34, 42, 45 (top), 49, 50, 51, 59
Andrea Stephens – page 54

ISBN 185276930-0

Printed in Singapore by Craft Print.

© Folens (not copiable)

Contents

Introduction

The introduction of design and technology into the National Curriculum framework presented teachers with the opportunity to help children to combine their knowledge, skills and understanding from other subject areas into exciting, realistic and stimulating contexts for learning.

Through design-and-technology activities, children are encouraged to:
- recognise and explore people's needs
- develop ideas about how these might be met
- develop products that meet those needs.

(SCAA, 1995).

Design-and-technology activities are a challenge for classroom organisation and management. This book aims to support teachers' understanding of the vocabulary of the National Curriculum and to illustrate how opportunities can be created for children to develop capabilities. The efficient management and organisation of these activities, to maximise learning for all children, is high on every teacher's agenda. This handbook is designed to support classroom teachers and curriculum co-ordinators in this process.

Aims of the Handbook

This handbook simplifies, clarifies and interprets the statutory order for design and technology by presenting teachers with numerous ideas for delivering its different aspects. The handbook:
- contains a simple step-by-step guide to developing a whole school policy for design and technology, at Key Stages 1 and 2
- explains the nature of the skills, processes, materials, and knowledge and understanding that children should encounter through a scheme of work
- shows how to create a scheme of work for design and technology that is appropriate to the needs of children, and is progressive within and across the key stages.

The book helps teachers to meet children's needs in a practical manner, and gives examples of how to manage resources and organise the curriculum to maximise learning. It is designed to help the less confident or less experienced teacher to manage confidently the requirements of the D&T curriculum.

Schemes of work and a school policy

A school policy for design and technology is a statement of how the National Curriculum statutory orders will be met. This must include:

- a scheme of work for each year group, which covers the programmes of study (PoS)
- details of how the children will be assessed.

Most policies also include other aspects, such as:

- aims and philosophy – what learning outcomes the subject hopes to achieve
- resources – materials, equipment, staff expertise and curriculum support materials
- SEN – how differentiation will be achieved
- funding – capitation and distribution of resources
- INSET – needs analysis and staff development opportunities.

Developing a scheme of work

Schemes of work are an integral part of school policy. Creating comprehensive schemes of work for an individual year group or key stage is made easy when teachers work together.

A scheme of work could be constructed simply as a series of project sheets which are carefully mapped against the elements of the National Curriculum PoS. Many schools also find it useful to develop key stage overviews which clearly illustrate progression and continuity. Both methods are illustrated on pages 10 and 11.

Where are we now?
Audit: existing policies, schemes of work, present D&T curriculum, resources and time allocation.

Where do we want to be?
To have a clear and concise scheme of work that is regularly reviewed and flexible; to have a policy that allows for continuity, progression, breadth and balance.

How will be know when we have arrived?
Staff are operating the policy, governors and parents have all been involved.

How do we get there?
By collaborating with staff; using support where available (such as advisory service and existing literature). By building on and extending resources. By having a planned financial allocation.

Elements of a Scheme of Work

The National Curriculum Programme of Study for Design and Technology at Key Stages 1 and 2 (DFE, 1995) identifies three key elements that should be used to inform the planning of a scheme of work for each key stage.

Opportunities:
- types of Design and Technology activity

Designing skills:
- generating ideas
- developing and communicating ideas
- planning
- evaluating.

Making skills:
- measuring and marking out
- cutting and shaping
- joining and combining
- finishing.

Knowledge and understanding of:
- materials and components
- mechanisms and control
- products and applications
- quality, health and safety and vocabulary.

Examples of schemes of work are given on pages 10 and 11.

Writing a whole-school policy

Philosophy

A suitable statement that reflects the aims of the school is required. For example:

'Design and technology can offer our pupils the opportunity to engage creatively with the made world. In a technological world people need to feel that they can understand and control the quality of products and applications of technology. To facilitate this, our pupils will undertake activities to develop their capability in ...'

Preparing to write a policy

A policy not founded in current practice will be of little practical use. You will need to begin by auditing the current practical activities undertaken within each year group. Identify those that could be considered as contributing to children's design-and-technology experience, for example the greetings cards and class books that they make, or the display they make of their own work. Record these activities under the topics or subject area in which they occur.

The purpose of this exercise is to enable the identification of gaps and any unnecessary overlap and repetition. Record this existing provision.

Having completed this exercise you are then in a position to begin completing your own version of the two charts on pages 10 and 11. The first chart guides you in planning for and assessing a single design-and-technology activity; the second is an example of a detailed scheme of work for progression in using a specific material.

Review of existing activities which could contribute to pupils' D&T capability

Timing	Description of activity	Skills and knowledge	
Year 1 *3 hours*	With contributions from each child, the class makes a collage for display in the classroom. Context changes from year to year.	Cutting fabrics to shape. Using different glues. (*Needs more thought about the focused activities undertaken and the range of skills developed.*)	A variety of reclaimed fabrics, different types of glues
Year 2 *Term 2* *2 hours*	Making an Easter greetings card. Individual activity	There is little gain here from other similar activities in the year. (*We could introduce some linkage mechanisms?*)	Card, sugar paper, a variety of other materials suitable for collage effects
Year 3 *Term 1* *4 hours*	Making a model lighthouse. Based on the book **The lighthouse keeper's lunch** Group activity	Simple electrical circuits are investigated and put to use in this model. (*This has elements of focused activities and provides a good design-and-make assignment. We could include some mechanisms here for transporting the lunch?*)	Papier mâché, PVA glue, paints, cardboard and other reclaimed materials. Bulbs, buzzers, batteries, switches, connecting wire

Elements of a D&T policy

Managment: The Role of the Co-ordinator

Review:
- Periodically reviewing the provision and its documentation.
- Liaising with staff to provide courses suitable for staff expertise and resources.

Co-ordination:
- Developing a consistent approach throughout the school.
- Providing continuity between year groups.
- Maintaining assessment, recording and reporting systems.

Staff development and support:
- Advice.
- Encouragement.
- Arranging INSET sessions.
- Collaborative teaching.
- Keeping everyone up to date.

Resources:
- Organising resource availability.
- Ordering.
- Advising and monitoring safety issues.

Liaison:
- Communicate with the SMT.
- Communicate with parents.
- Advise on reporting to parents.
- Report to Governors.
- Communicate with the LEA and/or other support agencies.
- Participate in professional development opportunities provided by support agencies.

Assessment

The National Curriculum requires assessment of two elements of design and technology:
- Designing
- Making

The assessment will have to be based on children designing and making 3-D solutions to problems. They are expected to be involved and assessed as they undertake three types of tasks:
- Design and Make Assignments (DMAs).
- Focused Practical Tasks – skill and knowledge building.
- Investigation, Disassembly and Evaluation of products activities (IDEAs). *These will be linked to the first two types of activity.*

Suitable methods of recording children's progress need to be agreed with the staff. A variety of opportunities and areas of experience which contribute to their capability are illustrated on pages 15 and 16. Guidance on assessment, recording and retaining evidence of progression between levels can be found on pages 60–63.

Timing

How will the design and technology programme be timetabled? The Dearing subject group recommended 36 hours at KS1 and 45 hours at KS2. Will the provision be built into existing 'topic based' work or taught as a separate element? The topic approach will mean the amount of time devoted to it will need to be estimated. For 'stand-alone' sessions, a pattern will have to be agreed, for example 24 afternoon sessions or rotating groups of six children on alternate days over a two-week cycle throughout the year.

Safety

As one of the few practical subjects in the curriculum, design and technology presents a number of safety issues. The main areas of concern are the hazards presented by the use of tools and certain materials, and hygienic practice with the use of food. All staff will need to be aware of a common set of rules, which ideally are devised co-operatively and communicated to the children when appropriate.

Hazards and Risks

The terms 'hazard' and 'risk', used in the National Curriculum Order, have a common meaning but need to be specifically understood in the context of safety. All potentially dangerous tools and materials need to be assessed, and simple rules should be set in place that teachers and children can work with.

Hazard – the potential danger that a tool, material, process or appliance presents.

Risk – a judgement of the actual danger presented by the use of a tool, material process or appliance used in a particular context.

Example:
Hazard – craft knives have very sharp blades that could cause a deep cut or even sever a child's finger.

The school needs to undertake a risk assessment exercise to minimise the risks, while avoiding imparing the natural progress children must make in their use of tools.

Risk Assessment:
Rule – craft knives are not used until years 5 to 6.

Condition of use – Children are taught how to use a safety ruler and a cutting mat to cut thin sheet materials under close supervision. Only children who have 'passed' the teacher's 'safety test' are allowed to use the knife. They should only use the equipment in close proximity to the teacher. In this way the risks are minimised.

Safety with Food

The health and safety issues raised by the Food Safety Act 1990 will be dealt with through:
- permission letters to parents
- regular maintenance of equipment
- cleaning systems for food preparation areas
- rules on food purchase and storage
- training of helpers and staff development
- first aid procedures
- health, safety and hygiene rules for children
- rules on use and maintenence of appliances.

Safety with tools
There are no hard and fast rules for when to introduce particular tools and associated techniques. Some children will be more dexterous than others, and SEN issues will need to be considered. Tools present lower risks when the material being cut or drilled is held securely.

Progression with cutting tools:
- safety scissors
- junior hacksaw
- craft cutters
- a range of 'Olfa' cutters
- Gent's saw
- shaper saw
- art knife, cutting mat and safety rule
- craft knife (under supervision)

Holding materials:
- elastic bands and bulldog clips
- bolt-on vice
- bench hooks
- jigs
- fixed vice or 'Workmate'
- pliers

Progression with drilling tools:
- hole punch on paper
- card drill
- hand drill on a stand
- hand drill, freely held
- bradawl

Special Educational Needs

Design and technology offers exciting and stimulating learning experiences for all children if the environment is supportive and well planned. The school's policy should indicate the way in which the needs of all learners will be met through good practice in differentiation, as well as those with particular special educational needs.

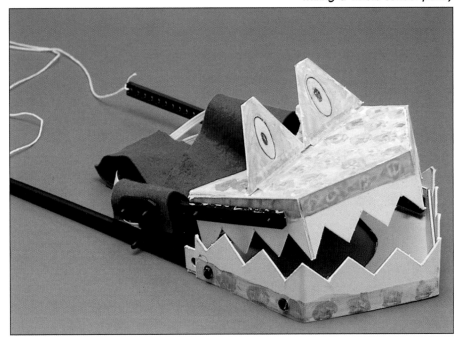

Differentiating activities

Focused tasks develop the understanding and skills of particular techniques, such as cutting, fixing and joining. The focused task and the design-and-make assignment will need to be closely related in time. Even simple tasks will need to be broken down into stages for which there are reinforcing outcomes.

Differentiation by task is essential in design-and-make assignments if all children are to gain in self-esteem and produce products that they can evaluate effectively. (See pages 54–55 on differentiated activities.)

Classroom practice for SEN

- Demonstrate techniques with children standing behind and to the side of you.
- Provide ambidextrous scissors.
- Use pre-marked materials for cutting.
- Use jigs and patterns for cutting.
- Support with planning procedural activities and making decisions when involved in the design process.
- Use memory prompts such as symbols to communicate processes.
- Display diagrams illustrating mechanisms and joining techniques.
- To assist communication, use computer resources such as overlay keyboards with words, materials and techniques to choose from.
- Use peer support – mixed ability groups.
- Use adult helpers:
  - Ensure that they understand the rationale for activities and strategies employed.
  - Let them supervise the majority of the class, releasing the teacher to work with SEN children.
  - Let them support individual children while undertaking a difficult or risky activity.
  - They could supervise a small group undertaking a particular task.

An equal opportunity policy

The whole school approach to the delivery of design and technology provides access to the curriculum for all children by:

- planning a curriculum that allows for some children working outside of their age-related key stage
- involving adult helpers and classroom assistants in planning for classroom activity
- specifying strategies to meet particular physical and learning needs in practical work
- allowing access to special resources.

The programme will need to be differentiated for age and ability.

Children with multiple learning needs may require a programme of experience focused around experimental work, providing a wide range of stimulating situations and experiences designed to facilitate the learning process.

Where practical activities are concerned, teachers often report problems of clumsiness and difficulties with fine motor skills. Recently, some of these children are being diagnosed as suffering from varying degrees of dyspraxia (often called 'clumsy child syndrome').

Design and Technology Scheme of Work

Year Group	Term	Duration

ACTIVITIES | PROGRAMMES OF STUDY

ACTIVITIES	Designing Skills	Making Skills	Knowledge and Understanding	Project Plan
Materials Food **Design and Make** Design and make a pizza for a specific given client group. **Identifying, Disassembling and Evaluating** Product evaluations of 5 breads: deciding criteria for evaluation and completing product evaluation sheet. **Focused Practical Tasks** Follow given recipes. Research different pizzas.	1. Product evaluation. 2. Specify client group for DMA and Test. 3. Complete specification and dietary requirements. 4. Evaluate products.	1. Follow recipes, checking measuring, combining and food process skills. 2. Produce a plan of action. 3. Log process and changes.	1. Health and safety practices with foods. 2. Understanding micro-organisms and mould and preservation. 3. Understand the processes of change in bread and manufacture and generalise from this.	**Stage One** 1. Evaluate 5 products, determining criteria for evaluation at start (some blind testing included). 2. Carry out tests and record results. 3. Complete product evaluation. **Stage Two** 1. Follow given recipe, Health and Safety guidelines. Make notes in log of what has been learned. **Stage Three** Adapt recipe for a client group. 1. Research the needs and preferences of this group. 2. Write out specification. 3. Adapt recipe and state stages in making. 4. Keep log of what you have done and changes made and why. 5. Make it and eat it. 6. Evaluate product and make critical supportive comments of the work of others. Suggest improvements to your own and what you would have done differently.

How to Assess

Observation of pupils and through discussion about their progress.

Using log books to see how much they plan, how they reflect on the changes and whether they have a clear plan of action.

The quality of their evaluations of their own work and of others, supportive comments, including comments on improvements.

What to Assess

1. Practical work and level of knowledge and independence and quality of outcome.
2. Developing a recipe for a client group and evaluating product against specification.
3. Knowledge and understanding of the programmes of study.

IT Opportunities

Make a flier or presentation of product for sale.

Resources

1. 5 different breads reflecting teacher choice.
2. Bread recipes, ingredients and equipment (oven, fridge, etc).
3. Product evaluation sheets.
4. Research materials on pizzas.
5. Dietary information.

Curriculum Links

science: changing materials

maths: measuring solids, fluids

health ed. English: critical reflective evaluation.

Vocabulary

Raising agents, preservation, micro-organism, moulds.

A PRIMARY TEACHER'S HANDBOOK – *Design and Technology*

© Folens (not copiable)

© Lewisham Professional Development Centre

Key Stage Planning Tool

Design and Technology Schemes of Work　**Mouldable Materials**　**Years (1–6)**

	KS1 (Years 1 & 2)	KS2 (Years 3 & 4)	KS3 (Years 5 & 6)
DMA Opportunities	Design and make shapes for a purpose, eg celebrations, jewellery (symbols and icons).	Design and make a large scale model of a mini-beast with one movement.	Masks and accessories for a carnival costume, eg headdress.
Focused Tasks	Skills of making and moulding shapes using chosen materials. Shaping techniques. Impressing. Applying and adding finishes. Joining to make jewellery.	Demonstrate how to cut and join materials. Experiment with adding texture. Demonstrate use of Modroc and papier mâché; use of tools for wire cutting.	Use of soldering iron to make support frame. Making framed structures in wire. Working with plastazote and papier mâché (cutting, marking and finishing).
IDEAS	Investigate jewellery for how it is made, finished and components used. Evaluate products.	Observation of mini-beasts and joints. Making drawings of whole and parts. Label drawings. Look at toys and models of similar 'beasts'.	Investigate products with particular focus on construction, joining, finishing and function. Conduct research from different sources.
Designing Learning Outcomes	Design shapes and how they will be combined for piece of jewellery. Decide who it is for. Evaluate the designs.	Design specification and brief including evaluation criteria at start. Label designs. Consider finishes. Propose a sequence of actions. Materials and equipment list. Evaluation.	Research, specify brief, produce a range of designs. Select the most appropriate, being aware of constraints. Designs labelled with dimensions. Evaluate work throughout.
Making Learning Outcomes	Make jewellery and talk about how it was made. Evaluate making process.	Measure, mark, cut and combine/join accurately. Apply movement and add components. Finish appropriately. Use materials efficiently with regard to waste. Evaluate practical outcome.	Step-by-step plan. Log of work to plan and any modifications made. Measuring more accurately, using tools with more precision.
Knowledge Learning Outcomes	Range and properties of mouldable materials. Production techniques (pouring, cutting, forming and shaping). Health and safety. Fitness for purpose. Quality.	Making structures (3-D) and combining with mouldable materials. How materials can be combined and mixed to create more useful properties. Structures.	Use of moulds to make further models, eg clay moulds, and making moulds to pour. Temperature at which plastizote becomes mouldable. When to use mouldable materials and where they are appropriate.
Assessment	Their drawings; their reflections on making. Who it is designed for and how well their designs work.	Pupils' self evaluations. Match between design and outcome. Range of ideas and quality of finished product. Ability to modify designs. Process diaries.	Process diaries; pupils' comments and observations. Teacher observation of process. Function and quality of aesthetics and manufacture of outcomes.
Differentiation	Level of challenge. Level of support and guidance. Type of questioning.	The complexity of model. Extension activities: different movements, adding circuits and switches	Level of task and support and guidance.
IT Opportunities	Drawing shapes on computer and changing colours and patterns.	Research CDs for information on mini-beasts. Scan in images to record work.	Multimedia presentation of costumes and process.
Resources	A selection of mouldable materials, components for jewellery. Examples of jewellery.	Papier mâché resources. Paint and varnish. Wire. Modroc. Wire cutters and pliers.	Plastazote. Soldering iron. Circular cutter. Wire. Heat source. Craft knives and mats. Wire mesh. Tool kits. Glue guns.
Vocabulary	Shapes, names of materials and techniques used.	Appropriate materials, manufacturing processes and tools.	Plastazote, moulds and mould-making terms. Framed structures.

© Lewisham Professional Development Centre

Design & technology in the National Curriculum

Key Stage 1

Mechanisms	Use simple mechanisms including wheels and axles, and joints that allow movement.	
Structures	Make their structures more stable and able to withstand greater loads.	
Products and applications	Investigate and disassemble simple products in order to learn how they function. Relate the ways things work to their intended purpose: how materials and components have been used, people's needs and what users say about them.	
Quality	Know that the quality of a product depends on how well it is made and how well it meets its purpose.	
Health and safety	Simple knowledge and understanding of health and safety, as consumers and when working with materials and components, including: – considering the hazards and risks in their activities – following simple instructions to control risk to themselves.	
Vocabulary	Use the appropriate vocabulary for naming and describing the equipment, materials and components they use.	

Key Stage 2

Materials and components	The characteristics of materials and their use: combining and mixing materials to create more useful properties.	
Control	How simple mechanisms can produce different types of movement. How to use electrical circuits usefully.	
Structures	How structures can fail when loaded, and techniques for reinforcing and strengthening them.	
Products and applications	To investigate, disassemble and evaluate simple products and applications to learn how they function. To relate the way things work to their intended purpose, how materials and components have been used, people's needs, and what users say about them.	
Quality	How well a product is made in terms of its purpose and the needs it meets.	
Health and safety	Control risks as designers, makers and consumers, including themselves and others.	
Vocabulary	To use the appropriate vocabulary for naming and describing the equipment, materials and components, and processes they use.	

Designing skills

	WHAT IT SAYS	WHAT IT MEANS
Key Stage 1	*The children should:* ✋ draw on their own experience to help generate ideas ✋ clarify their ideas through discussion ✋ develop their ideas through shaping, and assembling and rearranging materials and components ✋ develop and communicate their ideas by making freehand drawings, and by modelling their ideas in other ways, such as using actual materials and components with temporary fixings ✋ make suggestions about how to proceed ✋ consider their design ideas as these develop, identify strengths and weaknesses.	*D & M activity: toy/game. The child:* ✋ uses knowledge of own toys and games ✋ talks about toys and games generally ✋ selects and uses reclaimed materials and textiles to make a toy or game ✋ is capable of making simple free-hand drawings of what is to be made; arranges and rearranges materials ✋ talks about what they will do next ✋ is able to identify problems.
Key Stage 2	*The children should:* ✋ generate ideas, consider the users and purposes for which they are designing ✋ clarify ideas, develop criteria for their designs and suggest ways forward ✋ consider appearance, function, safety and reliability when developing proposals ✋ explore, develop and communicate their design proposals by modelling their ideas in a variety of ways ✋ develop a clear idea of what has to be done, propose actions and alternative methods if things go wrong ✋ evaluate their design ideas bearing in mind the users and the purposes for which the product is intended, and indicate ways of improving their ideas.	*The child:* ✋ is able to make a toy or game for a specific age range or to meet a particular need ✋ can discuss aspects of the toy or game in relation to the users' needs ✋ can take into account users' preferences in the design proposal ✋ is able to demonstrate design ideas in a number of ways, using a variety of materials when required to do so ✋ knows and understands what has to be done and can flexibly adapt the design plan as the need arises ✋ is able to discuss the original criteria in relation to the final product and talks about ways of improving the toy or game.

Programme of Study

Making skills

	WHAT IT SAYS	WHAT IT MEANS
Key Stage 1	*The children should:* ✋ select appropriate materials, tools and techniques ✋ measure, mark out, cut and shape a range of materials ✋ assemble, join, combine materials and components ✋ apply simple finishing techniques ✋ make suggestions about how to proceed ✋ evaluate their products as these are developed, identifying strengths and weaknesses.	*D & M activity: toy/game. The child:* ✋ chooses items from a limited range ✋ uses non-standard measures and simple cutting and shaping techniques ✋ randomly attaches materials without considering aesthetics ✋ uses paint or fabric for example to cover a product ✋ explains what will happen next ✋ talks about problems when questioned but makes no changes.
Key Stage 2	*The children should:* ✋ select appropriate materials, tools and techniques ✋ measure, mark out, cut and shape a range of materials, using additional tools, equipment and techniques ✋ join and combine materials and components accurately in temporary and permanent ways ✋ apply additional finishing techniques appropriate to the materials being used and the purpose of the product ✋ develop a clear idea of what has to be done, planning how to use materials, equipment and processes, and suggesting alternative methods of making ✋ evaluate their products, identifying strengths and weaknesses, and carrying out appropriate tests ✋ implement improvements they have identified.	*The child:* ✋ thoughtfully makes a selection based upon considered criteria ✋ uses standard measures with an extended range of tools, equipment and techniques, for example a measuring jug or a ruler ✋ is able to accurately attach materials to each other ✋ considers appearance and user preferences ✋ is able to plan for the different stages of making ✋ talks generally about the toy or game, demonstrating successes and shortcomings ✋ modifies the design and takes account of any problems which arise.

Providing opportunities

The National Curriculum describes a number of opportunities that should be presented to children to enable them to develop their design-and-technological capability. In the following pages the nature of these opportunities are developed with suggestions for specific classroom activities.

In this book we have described **opportunities** as the 'types' of activity in which children will be involved, for example 'design and make assignments'. The experiences with different materials and components, for example textiles, food stuff and flexible materials, we have called **areas of experience**. The diagram below shows the relationship between these two components and the elements of design-and-technology capability.

		OPPORTUNITIES		
		Design-and-Make Assignments	Focused Practical tasks	Investigate, disassemble and evaluate tasks
AREAS OF EXPERIENCE	Materials and Components	*Designing skills* *Making skills* *Knowledge & Understanding*		

Opportunities

Investigate, disassemble and evaluate activities (IDEAs)	Typical activity
Children should be provided with opportunities to explore existing products to: 🖑 investigate their properties 🖑 disassemble them to see how they are constructed 🖑 evaluate the quality of products.	A common D&T task is to make a greetings card for a particular event or celebration. It offers plenty of opportunity for differentiation by task, since at a simple level it can be a collage, and more able children can include mechanisms. Children investigate a collection of different cards, including ones with moving parts, made for different purposes and occasions. They identify the materials they are made from and see how they work. A class survey is used to find out which cards members of the class like.
Focused Practical Tasks (FPTs)	
Children should be provided with opportunities to develop and practise: 🖑 aspects of knowledge and understanding 🖑 a range of specific skills.	Children should be shown and practise how to: 🖑 cut accurately to marked-out lines 🖑 score and fold paper 🖑 produce a block of text on a computer 🖑 change the font if necessary 🖑 create a display of simple folds and linkages to make moving parts 🖑 describe the properties of a range of flexible materials.
Design-and-make assignments (DMAs)	
Children should be provided with opportunities to design and make products that: 🖑 meet real needs 🖑 draw on their repertoire of skills 🖑 work in relevant contexts to their abilities.	Children investigate a particular celebration such as Christmas, Easter or Diwali. They gather a range of symbols representative of the event. Using their previous knowledge, they design a card for a named person. Ideas are developed by discussion, then through sketches and simple paper models. These are kept as part of a design diary. Children choose from a range of materials and techniques that they are aware of. During making, the quality of the card is an important factor. Comments from the recipient are added to the design diary.

(Left margin heading: Opportunities)

Areas of experience: designing skills

Generating ideas

Problem solving

Problem Solving

The children may be required to solve a 'real life' problem, or can be presented with one in the context of a story or other fictional situation, such as:

- How could Humpty Dumpty be helped so that he will stay on the wall?
- Teddy needs a swing for the garden. Can you make one?
- Can you find the quickest and safest way of transporting an egg between two tables?

Children of all ages can appreciate the challenge of this type of problem-solving exercise.

Different ways of generating ideas

Ideas for design and make activities should be placed within a meaningful context. There are many interesting ways in which ideas for design-and-technology activities can be generated. Generally, ideas for designs are generated as a result of some form of aural or visual stimulus, such as:

- stories, poems and nursery rhymes, for example *The Three Bears, Hey Diddle Diddle*
- pictures and illustrations, for example books, magazines, comics and posters
- plays and drama, for example books, television and radio
- special events and celebrations, for example birthday celebration cards and holidays
- product evaluation, for example toys, games, comics, sportswear and food products
- problem solving and investigation activities, for example real and hypothetical.

Investigations

Investigating needs, wants and preferences can also be a source of ideas for design and make activities:

- Design a celebration cake for a football fan.
- What would the cake look like?
- What would it be made from?
- How would it be decorated?

Product analysis

Consumer preferences can be addressed through discussion or by using simple questioning techniques. Older children can design questionnaires to gather answers to their own questions. After all, children express their opinions on numerous products ranging from sweets and chocolates, food generally, clothes, toys and games. They are also capable of discussing value for money and quality in relation to many products.

Getting the balance right

Ideas can originate from cross-curricular topics or projects. However, to enable the children to be given breadth and depth in their designing and making experiences, it is essential that the type of opportunities they are given reflect different areas of the design and technology curriculum. It is essential that the children work with a variety of materials, tools and equipment and not just a limited range within the area specified by the National Curriculum.

By drawing upon their past experiences of products, children can be encouraged not only to generate design ideas but also to evaluate them. Previous experience of investigating, disassembling and evaluating products will help the children to generate ideas for design. These ideas should be developed through discussion, therefore allowing them to proceed to achieve their own realistic design outcomes.

Developing and communicating ideas

Design ideas are only useful if they can be developed and communicated to others. Professional designers use a variety of communication skills to convey their ideas, and children of all ages should be taught to use similar skills and techniques.

There are three main skill areas that relate to developing and communicating ideas.

My design idea

NAME Francesca

My idea is to make......
a puppet

It should ......
move its arms

It should not .....

This is what it should look like

I will need....
pins
card
wool
lolly stick

It was good because...

It was not so good because....

To make it better I would ....

Speaking and listening skills	✋ talking ✋ using the language of design and technology in context ✋ discussing – exploring, developing and explaining ideas ✋ sharing ideas, insights and opinions ✋ questioning, planning, predicting and investigating ✋ evaluating ✋ oral reporting – describing events and observations ✋ recommending – presenting to audiences
Practical skills	✋ shaping ✋ assembling ✋ rearranging ✋ modelling ✋ pictures and illustrations ✋ freehand drawing ✋ sketches ✋ labelled sketches
Writing skills	✋ planning – notes, flow charts ✋ drafting – developing ideas from plan into structured, written text ✋ revising – altering and improving the draft ✋ proof-reading – checking the draft ✋ presenting – preparing for final copy ✋ using different types of written communication

　　　© Folens (not copiable)

Various forms of written communication exist. Different types are required at various stages throughout the design-and-make process, including:

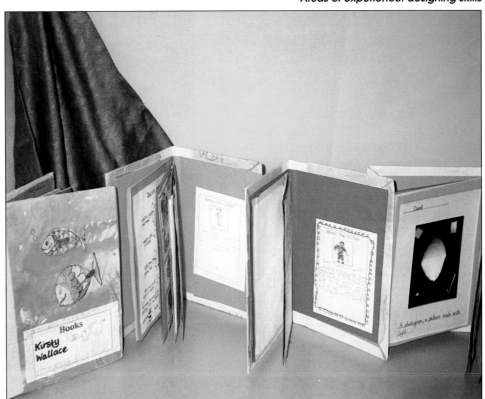

- **notes** – abbreviated text
- **scripts** – general writing
- **diaries** – sequencing and cataloguing events
- **reports** – activity progress logs
- **instructions** – systematic lists and guides
- **explanations** – detailed accounts.

Progression

The age and ability of the children will determine the content, style and extent to which their written communication skills are developed.

It is essential that their work is systematically collected and collated. As their skills develop, they will be able to compile their own portfolios. However, suitable arrangements should be made to store the work of younger children.

Progression in developing and communicating ideas:

Talk about familiar products, for example hats, food, toys.

Can assemble materials into a product and explain their decisions in simple terms.

Make simple 2-D sketches to describe their 3-D products.

Represent design ideas with freehand drawings and some limited technical words before making them.

Evaluate a product using sketches and words.

Use labelled sketches to describe design ideas.

Make 3-D models to explore design ideas, for example using a construction kit.

Make short presentations to the class using models and sketches to illustrate ideas.

© Folens (not copiable)

Planning

Planning requires children to structure and sequence design-and-technology activities, so that successful outcomes can be achieved. They should be taught to use different types of planning tools and they should be encouraged to adopt a variety of planning strategies at various stages throughout the designing-and-making process. Effective planning strategies should take into account the materials, tools and equipment that are available and how much time there is to complete each task.

The cost associated with each activity should also be considered. Activities that emphasise acknowledging the cost of materials should be incorporated into the design and technology curriculum.

It is essential that the skills, knowledge and understanding each child brings to a task is recognised, as prior learning plays a significant role in calculating how much time should be allocated to each stage of the design-and-make process. If new skills are to be learned, teachers should recognise that time will have to be allocated for this purpose.

Planning tools and ideas

- **Brainstorming** – talking, discussing and recording individual tasks.
- **Analysis** – breaking down the requirements.
- **Group analysis** – collectively finding out what is required.
- **Thumbnail sketches** – using words and simple pictures to illustrate stages.
- **Check lists** – recording and checking what has been, and what is to be, achieved.
- **Flow charts** – showing development through different stages.
- **Lists** – details of requirements.
- **Diaries** – dated sequence of events schedule.
- **Log books** – recording what has been done – during and after the task.

Tools for planning

It is essential that young children are gradually helped towards creating their own design-and-technology 'sequence of activity' schedules, as carefully planned tasks allow them to proceed through different designing-and-making stages with ease. Older children should be able to make and use their own planning schedules. Time-plans can help the children structure their work.

Time-plans

Time-plans give the children a framework in which to organise their work in relation to materials, tools and equipment and, where appropriate, associated costs. By breaking down the activity into separate parts, the children will be able to monitor their own progress and assess how much they have achieved within a given period.

Children at Key Stage 1 should have their time and resources monitored by the teacher. The children should be prompted at regular intervals to ensure that they are on schedule or on target to completing a specific task successfully. The time intervals should be based around non-standard time measures, such as finishing before playtime or by the end of the school day.

A PRIMARY TEACHER'S HANDBOOK – *Design and Technology* © Folens (not copiable)

Children at Key Stage 2 should be encouraged to devise their own time-plans and take control of their work patterns. At this stage they may be able to organise their work into hourly patterns or they may be able to plan over a longer period of time. For example, children working on a project that lasts for a number of sessions, either through the week or over a half term, should create a simple date-planner.

Planning for materials, tools and equipment

The children must plan which resources they will require and indicate the quantity of the materials they need.

Problems will arise if they do not identify their production needs, as other children may use the materials they require and this can have a major impact upon the final product. It is important that the children learn that the quality of any product is dependent upon the materials from which it is made. Within the classroom a limited number of resource materials are available, and these are generally shared among the children taking part in the activities. They should be encouraged to consider their needs and the needs of the other children.

Costs

The children should be encouraged to consider the cost of the materials they are using and the influence the cost will have upon the design-and-make process and the quality of the final product.

There are a number of ways in which even young children can be helped with this process:

- They could select a limited number of materials from an extensive range of materials but they can select freely from reclaimed materials.

- They could manage a 'budget' for their design-and-make artefact. They can, for example, be given a fictitious amount of money, such as 20p, and from this amount they choose from carefully labelled areas of materials for sale at 2p or 5p, and so on. The costs can be made more realistic with the age and ability of the children.

Progression in planning

Talks about what is being/will be done when prompted.

Talks about ideas and what is to be done.

Discusses ideas and answers questions appropriately.

Makes realistic suggestions about what will be done and how it will be achieved.

Evaluates work as it progresses and accommodates plans to meet required changes.

Carefully creates and modifies plans where necessary.

Areas of experience: making skills

It is essential for children to develop skills that will enable them to measure and mark out their designs accurately, using a variety of different materials. Measuring and marking materials has a direct impact upon their ability to assemble resources and to realise their final product. Similarly, their ability to use patterns in their designs enables efficient use of materials and therefore limits the cost of the resources.

Specific types of materials demand different measuring and marking techniques. Patterns can generally be used effectively on stiff and flexible sheet material. A variety of tools and equipment can also help children to achieve greater accuracy in this process.

The children should be encouraged to use and develop a range of measuring and marking-out techniques, including:

- **templates** – patterns used to reproduce shapes
- **stencils** – devices for applying designs
- **motifs** – a recurring shape in a design
- **patterns** – a plan or diagram used as a guide in making something
- **pattern arrangements** – random or systematic.

The children should also be able to demonstrate their measuring and marking ability through:

- **lay outs** – preliminary plans
- **mock-ups** – scaled models
- **blueprints** – original plans of a prototype (prototype – an original model from which improved types can be made – an example of a type)
- **models** – representations on a smaller scale
- **moulds** – formed shapes.

Progression in measuring and marking out

There are several ways in which children can be helped to achieve accuracy in their making activities, such as organising them into mixed ability groups. For example, children with different measuring and marking-out skills can work together to produce a satisfactory outcome. However, children with specific needs should be given appropriate adult support to ensure that they are satisfied with the work they are undertaking.

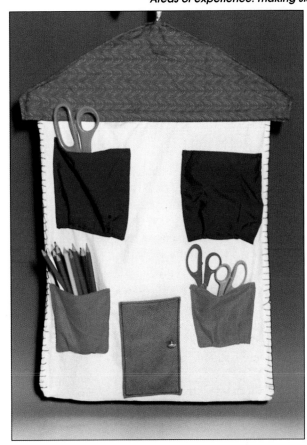

Younger or less able children should be taught to use non-standard measures, such as:

- **food** – spoons and cups for measuring ingredients rather than weighing scales
- **textiles** – wooden rods cut to a specific length as measurement guides – therefore removing the need for the children to be able to read accurately standard measures for length, such as the centimetre
- **stiff and flexible sheet materials** – making paper patterns and templates before stiff or flexible sheet materials (such as wood or fabric) are cut can help children to decide if they need to make any last minute changes to their design.

As the children progress they should be able to demonstrate greater accuracy in their measuring and marking skills. They should be encouraged to use standard measuring tools and equipment that are appropriate to specific materials, such as:

- **food** – measuring spoons and jugs, kitchen scales
- **textiles** – tape measures
- **stiff and flexible sheet materials** – ruler, tri-squares.

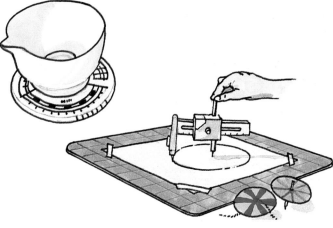

Cutting & Shaping

The way in which materials are cut and shaped has a direct influence on the assembly process and the overall look of the final product. It is essential that the children learn to use materials, tools and equipment in a safe and appropriate way in order that the quality of their products can be maximised.

It is important to remember that any cutting tool or equipment in the classroom can be potentially dangerous if used in an inappropriate way; a sharp pencil can be just as dangerous as blunt scissors if used carelessly. It is also worth noting that specific materials require tools to be reasonably sharp; it is very difficult to be accurate when cutting and shaping if the tool being used is blunt or unsuitable for the task. Using blunt or inappropriate tools can be very frustrating for the children, as their expectations cannot be met. Specific items of clothing should be worn where appropriate and surface areas covered and protected.

There are simple ways in which materials can be shaped, and a variety of tools and equipment have been designed to enable children of all ages to support specific materials during the cutting and shaping stages. Progression and accuracy in cutting and shaping is a gradual process, and the children's development will depend upon the types of opportunities they are given to work with a wide range of resources.

Technology Teaching Systems (TTS) has an excellent range of cutting and shaping tools and equipment. See page 64 for details.

Progression in cutting and shaping

Generally, children's ability to use specific tools and equipment for cutting and shaping a variety of material depends upon their exposure to specific resources.

Scissors are the main cutting tool used by children in the primary classroom. However, becoming an 'expert' or progressing using only scissors is unacceptable.

To enable them to progress, appropriate equipment for cutting and shaping should be made available and teachers should ensure that they are used safely.

The following guide to tools and equipment illustrates the range of resources that are available for cutting and shaping. Protective items are also listed.

Tools and equipment for food and textiles

Food
- aprons
- chopping board
- cutting mats
- food grater
- French peeler
- juice extractor
- masher
- pastry cutter and stainless steel 'shape' cutters
- rolling pin
- sieve
- spreader
- strainer
- vegetable knife
- vegetable peeler

Textiles
- fabric frames
- fabric scissors
- leather punch
- pinking shears
- weaving looms

Tools for cutting and shaping card and paper

Cutting straight lines and curves
- **Perforation cutter** – creates a perforated line on paper or thin card.
- **Quick cutter** – the blade hardly protrudes so will not cut fingers. Useful with card and paper.
- **Safety snips** – for general use.
- **Wavy cutter** – cuts wavy lines on card, paper and felt.
- **Edging scissors** – cuts decorative edges on card and paper.

Making holes
- **Handy punch** – makes 5mm holes in card.
- **Paper drill and cutter** – holes in card or sheets of corrugated plastic.

- **Single hole punch** – 6mm holes in card.
- **Bradawl** – small holes.

Tools for stiff and flexible sheet materials

Wood: *equipment to improve cutting and shaping techniques.*
- basic bench hooks
- G-clamps
- small swivel vice
- mitre-blocks
- drillstand, drill jig
- Wilson blocks

Wood: *cutting and shaping tools.*
- saws – junior hacksaw, coping saw, tenon saw and gent's low-voltage fretsaw
- sandpaper
- files – round and flat

Wood: *making holes*
- small handrill and a variety of bits
- Abra file

© Folens (not copiable)

Joining and combining

The types of resources made available to the children will obviously determine the joining and combining techniques they select. Generally, resources for joining and combining are material specific.

The quality of any final design and make product is directly influenced by the techniques used to attach and join the different materials together.

Unfortunately, some potentially good products are ruined by children selecting a glue that is inappropriate for use with the materials they have elected to use.

Problems arise when materials and attachment techniques are incompatible, however there are a number of ways to effectively join and combine a variety of different materials.

To attach or join specific materials securely and effectively, it may be necessary to use temporary attachment techniques first. The advantage of using this form of attachment or joining technique is that it enables the children to make any changes that are required prior to joining the materials permanently.

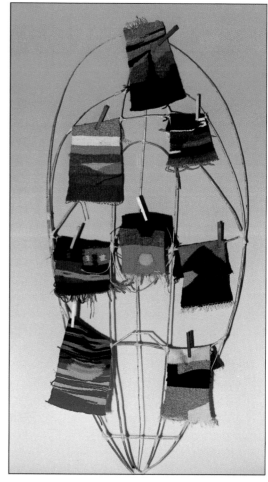

Temporary attachment resources

- masking tape
- clothes pegs
- paper fasteners
- Velcro ®
- Blu-Tack ®
- Linx jointers – used to create 90 degree angles
- string

Progression in joining and combining

As the children progress through the key stages, they will develop the ability to select the appropriate resources to join and combine materials.

Younger or less able children should be given the opportunity to select from a limited range of materials so that they can develop their knowledge and understanding of the different properties of materials. If children are never allowed to make a selection their repertoire of making skills will be limited.

To help them join and combine materials effectively, focused practical tasks should be specifically designed to extend their knowledge and understanding.

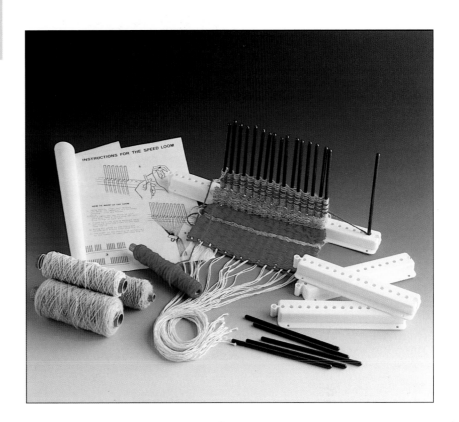

Tools and equipment for food and textiles

Food
- rotary whisks
- mixing spoons and bowls
- mashers
- spreaders

Textiles:
- needles and thread
- weaving loom
- Copydex
- eyelet punch
- Velcro strips
- elastic
- assorted fasteners including: hooks and eyes, zips, laces, safety pins, buttons, ribbon, snap fasteners, buckles
- Binca cross stitch fabric
- perforated paper
- Image maker – to create a transfer

Tools and equipment for stiff and flexible sheet materials

Stiff and flexible sheet materials:
- Linx jointers
- eyelet punch pliers
- screws
- staples
- balsa cement
- clothes pegs
- washers – to keep axles in place
- thick card axle supports
- card fastenings, including treasury tags, pipe cleaners, brass paper fasteners and paper binders
- soft wire
- corrugated plastic sheet joiners such as corri-joiners, click rivets and waterproof tape

finishing

It would be wrong to assume that the way in which a product will be finished should be left until the final stages of making. Finishing should be considered during the designing-and-making process, as it will have a direct influence upon the way in which the product is finally produced. It will also affect the materials that are used in the design.

Different materials and techniques can be used to create very effective and attractive finishes. They can enhance a range of products made from different types of materials.

Techniques and equipment for food and textiles

Food
The following are a few examples of the ways in which food can be finished.

- icing buns
- dressing salads
- glazing chicken
- decorating cakes
- coating with bread crumbs
- covering with sauce
- trimming with garnish

Textiles
Numerous resources are available for children to finish products made from textiles attractively. Specific skills may need to be addressed when introducing unfamiliar techniques such as dying or printing. They should also be involved in selecting the most appropriate joining techniques that will enhance the selected finishing materials.

- beads
- colour fun glossy paints
- cold water dye
- Colour fun glitter paints
- Colour fun paints
- Colour fun dyesticks
- coloured match sticks
- fabric crayons
- feathers
- Fabric fun water colour dyes
- Image maker: acts as a transfer on to fabric
- Lurex thread
- reflective pattern sheets
- screen printing
- sequins

Progression in finishing

It is impossible to determine linear progression in finishing. The children's experiences will support their learning about finishing techniques and teachers should take every opportunity to allow them to extend their knowledge using a variety of materials.

In order for them to gain valuable knowledge and understanding, they should be taught to assess different types of finishing techniques. They will need to develop their ability to analyse the needs, wants and preferences of the consumer.

They should also be presented with appropriate materials, tools and equipment to finish the products they have effectively designed and made. They should be helped to assess the quality of their own work and the work of professionals.

They should to be taught to appreciate that the finish of a product might not reflect its overall quality, and that some finishes are designed to prevent the purchaser from identifying flaws in the product.

Discuss value for money, to enable them to grasp the concept that financial constraints affect the manufacturer as well as the purchaser.

Ceramic food which has been painted and glazed.

Techniques for stiff and flexible sheet materials

Stiff- and flexible-sheet materials and reclaimed materials

Aiming to create a pleasing effect can present children with challenging situations, particularly when sheets of plastic or plastic product containers have been incorporated into a design.

The ability to select the right finishing techniques is vital to the overall look of the product. It is also important for the children to consider 'wear and tear' on the product if it is to remain attractive or serviceable.

When working with stiff and flexible sheet materials and reclaimed materials a number of approaches should be considered including:

- **cladding** – using papier mâché
- **framing** – with wood and other construction materials
- **painting** – using different types mixed with or without PVA
- **patterning** – marbling, transfers
- **sanding** – to smooth the surface area
- **staining** – vegetable dyes and other suitable products
- **texturing** – paper by attaching other materials
- **varnishing** – using PVA
- **waxing** – coating the surface of card or paper to make it water resistant
- **stenciling** – to create decorative effects

Areas of experience: designing & making skills

Evaluation skills are required throughout the designing-and-making process, and it is essential that children progressively develop the ability to evaluate their work objectively. They need to develop specific skills so that they can reflect on their ideas, suggest improvements and make judgements about the outcomes of their work and the work of others, including professional designers. There are ways in which they can demonstrate their ability to evaluate. As they progress through experience and structured opportunities, their ability to evaluate effectively throughout the designing-and-making process will develop.

The three puppets can each be evaluated in different ways. The stick puppet might be favoured because it is cheap to make or easy to use. Alternatively, one of the more complicated puppets might be suitable for a more capable child.

Designing and making

Evaluation: designing skills
The children should be taught to:
- collect information from a variety of sources
- address conflicting requirements
- explain users' preferences
- demonstrate understanding as to how the product will be used
- use a variety of criteria to develop a design proposal.

Evaluation: making skills
The children should be taught to:
- explain why they are making something
- demonstrate why materials or techniques have been selected
- assess the quality of their final product
- compare their product to the original plan
- identify what has worked well
- make recommendations
- adjust making techniques to improve quality
- adapt making plans to improve quality, safety and economy.

Progression in Evaluating

Children adapt and adjust their designs naturally as they handle materials. As they progress, their designing-and-making skills develop and they are able to plan to design and make in a more systematic and efficient way.

Initially, teachers need to encourage them to describe their thinking verbally:

- by responding to appropriate questions posed by the teacher
- by discussing the reasons for their choices.

By thinking in this way, they are evaluating. It is important to remember that written evaluation schedules can be constraining on children's natural ability.

They can be encouraged gradually to write reports on their designing-and-making experiences, but the nature and complexity of the report will vary depending on the type of activity and the age range of the children.

Evaluating successfully the products they design and make depends on the quality of the design specification to which they are working. Fitness for purpose is the way in which quality is defined, and it is this that provides the criteria by which they will evaluate their work.

A child's early experiences of planning, designing and making should result in simple, staightforward products.

Useful evaluation techniques

- **Choosing** – which do you like the best?
- **Ranking** – place in order of preference.
- **Rating** – score out of 10.
- **Classify** – sort into different categories.
- **Testing** – does it do what it is supposed to do?
- **Fair testing** – change one variable at a time, keeping everything else the same.
- **Market research** – ask others what they prefer.
- **User tips** – ask a user to try out the product and report back.
- **Trial and error** – make gradual changes to improve product.

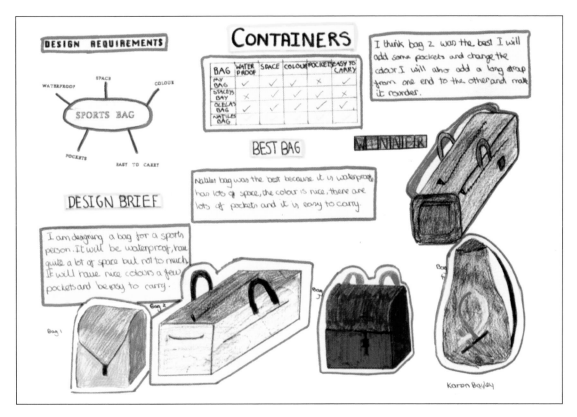

Knowledge and understanding

Design and technology offers children the opportunity to work with a wide range of materials and components. They will have encountered many of the materials in their everyday lives but will not understand why they are used and how the particular properties of a material or component fits it for that purpose. At Key Stage 1, children are not required to have knowledge and understanding in this area. However, even the youngest children can be encouraged to discuss why they are using a particular material in their design. Working with different materials and components is explored in more depth on pages 44–53.

What it says	What it means
Key Stage 1	
(2a) Work with a range of materials and components, including sheet materials, items that can be assembled to make products, *eg reclaimed materials*, textiles, food and construction kits. **(2b)** Investigate how the working characteristics of materials can be changed to suit different purposes. **(4a)** ... select materials (making skills) **(5d)** ... to relate the way things work to their intended purpose, how materials and components have been used, people's needs and what users say about them.	Work with a range of reclaimed materials such as paper, card, plastics and some metal. Selecting from the available materials, children combine them together to make structures, products or models of products. They talk about the properties of the materials in terms of being stiff, clear, soft, shiny, bendy and so on. Use card to reinforce paper or textile products, stuffing to stiffen textiles, weave materials together to make a wall hanging, blend food ingredients, use chocolate to join dry ingredients together, explaining the properties with appropriate vocabulary.
Key Stage 2	

(2a) Work with a range of materials and components, including stiff and flexible sheet materials, materials that are suitable for making frameworks, mouldable materials, textiles, food, electrical and mechanical components and construction kits.
 	
 (5a) be taught... how the working characteristics of materials relate to the way materials are used.
 (5b) be taught... how materials can be combined and mixed in order to create more useful properties
	Make frameworks from wood that are clad with card from reclaimed boxes to make strong structures, such as house, bridges and furniture.
	   Make the base of a mask from mouldable foam and relate how the properties of the material changed on heating and cooling.
	   Explain how to make a variety of bread rolls with different textures and finishes using a flour and water mixture and yeast.
	   When making frameworks from wood clad with card from reclaimed boxes, be able to describe the role of the framework and the cladding in strengthening the structure.

Progression in using materials and components

Note: This progression is presented as a guide only. It is important to remember that progression is not always linear and that children could be working at many of these stages according to their prior experiences or the learning opportunities presented to them.

Makes simple fantasy structures for story characters using reclaimed materials and explains why they have chosen the shapes and types of material in their design.

Nursery/Reception

Uses a construction kit and becomes familiar with the different types of components and their functions.

Knows how to strengthen paper and card by rolling, folding and corrugating to make structures.

Knows a number of ways of stiffening fabric.

Can explain how to change the taste and texture of bread mixes.

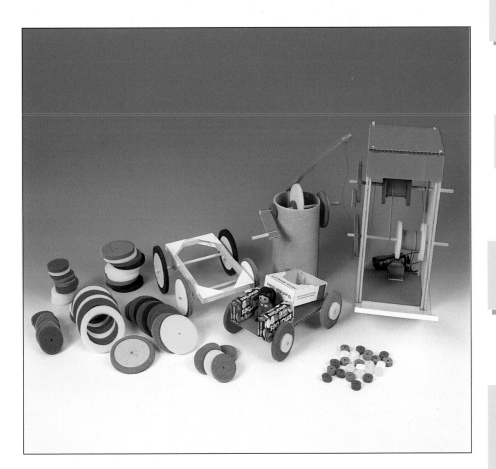

Makes a simple vehicle from resistant materials and a source of power. The annotated sketch explains the function of the wheel, axles, motor and gears from which it is made.

Makes a reading tent for the classroom to explain the principles that make the structure strong.

Weaves a variety of materials together to explain how they will effect the finished product.

Year 6

Uses a technical construction kit which contains a 'control box' to build a model of a lift.

Makes a range of 'healthy' biscuits and explains how the different ingredients contribute to a healthy diet.

Mechanisms & Control

Mechanisms and Control

The foundations of experience with a range of mechanisms are laid in the primary school years. Understanding some of the basic principles will help to highlight aspects of the mechanisms that children investigate and to assist them in their problem-solving activities.

Opportunities

Construction kits (see pages 50-51) offer children a simple way of experimenting with mechanisms and control. The concepts explored with kits can be transferred to work with mechanical and electrical components and frameworks as they become more skilled at making.

Experience with electrical circuits in science lessons will be a useful experience to draw on.

Examination of a variety of everyday tools and devices will provide a rich context to draw on for ideas.

TAKE A RIDE INTO SPACE Only £2·50

Principles

Machines

A device that changes the size or direction of a force is termed a 'machine'. The simplest machines are levers. A lever is a rigid object through which a force can be transferred around a pivot. A screwdriver opening a tin of paint is an example of a lever. The different types of lever describe where the forces act in relation to the pivot. Linkages are usually straight pieces of rigid material linked together through mobile joints.

- spanners
- pliers
- fishing rods
- scissors
- cranks

Gears

Gears are a series of toothed wheels (cogs) which, while changing the speed of motion, can also change the force applied. Gears can also be linked by a chain drive.

- car gearbox
- bicycle wheel and chain
- fishing reel
- rotary egg whisk.

Pulleys

Pulleys have the same principles as gears in terms of changing speed and force but the link between the wheels is flexible – a belt instead of teeth. A belt link is useful because it can allow for some slipping if forces are applied quickly, and is less precise than toothed wheels which need to be fitted together carefully.

Pneumatics and hydraulics

Linking two syringes with a piece of flexible tubing allows the size, direction and point of application of a force to be changed. Air-filled tubes are pneumatic, fluid-filled are hydraulic. The latter are more positive in their action because the fluid cannot be compressed.

- excavators (hydraulics)
- automatic doors (pneumatics)

Wheels and axles

Allow for low friction movement.

- cars
- buggies
- bicycle
- pulleys
- wheelbarrow

Progression in using mechanisms and Control

Note: This progression is presented as a guide only. It is important to remember that progression is not always linear and that children could be working at many of these stages according to their prior experiences or the learning opportunities presented to them at earlier stages.

Describes the movement of toys and other simple mechanisms using familiar vocabulary.

Nursery/Reception

Understands the need for a sequence of commands to control a floor robot.

Is able to describe simple mechanical devices, eg door handles.

Can construct simple mechanisms from construction kits and point out the different components.

Can describe how linkages can change the direction of movement when making a puppet.

Knows how to use syringes and plastic tubing to transfer movement.

Uses electric motors, syringes and tubing to transfer linear movement.

Selects wheels, pulleys, belts and gears when producing mobile vehicles.

Can write a sequence of commands on the computer to control a model.

Introduces axles and wheels into their design when making a vehicle.

Can describe simple ideas about the behaviour of familiar mechanisms such as bicycles, whisks, adjustable spanners.

Year 6

Selects from a variety of electrical components such as bulbs, buzzers, batteries, switches when constructing electrical circuits.

Structures

Structures

Many teachers will have experienced children building structures from reclaimed materials, such as cardboard boxes, or making towers from rolled up newspapers. The principles of structures are found in variety of contexts, from an egg box to a multi-storey building. Children can undertake focused tasks to investigate structures, such as:

- 👋 **furniture** – tables, chairs, beds and cupboards
- 👋 **containers** – packaging for transit
- 👋 **playground furniture** – carousel, climbing frame and swings
- 👋 **places to live** – tents, shelters, huts, houses and flats
- 👋 **bridges and towers** – drawbridge, suspension bridge, Roman arch, pylons, and cranes

- 👋 **construction kits** – can give early success and allow principles of structures to be experienced and learned: Lego, Plawco, Brio, Reo click and Meccano
- 👋 **stiff, flexible and reclaimed materials** – bottles, boxes, paper, card and cardboard, wood and corrugated plastics.

Principles

Although most structures are made from rigid materials such as steel, wood, plastic and cardboard, they are designed to deform when forces are applied to them. When a material bends or stretches, internal forces are set up which balance the force being applied. The structure is said to be in equilibrium; the forces are balanced. If the structure cannot balance the force being applied it is overloaded, and then it will fail and fall down.

Types of structure
- 👋 **Shell** – a thin outer covering which is normally self-supporting, such as cardboard packaging or an egg box.
- 👋 **Frame** – a structure made up of individual elements, such as a climbing frame made of aluminium tubing or a timber-framed house.
- 👋 **Shell and frame** – a framework clad with an outer shell, such as a tent or a steel-frame building.

- 👋 **Stabilising** – adding weights to the bottom of a structure
  - props and ties – a tent
  - tapering – increasing the size of the base
  - fixing the base to a solid object.
- 👋 **Strengthening and reinforcing**
  - making a material behave as though it was stronger
  - folding and rolling
  - cladding with a shell of stiff materials
  - corner joints
  - bracing with struts and ties.

- 👋 **Testing** – fair testing, controlling variables
  - loading – adding weights until the structure bends or breaks
  - pushing and pulling – use a forcemeter to find how many newtons it takes to make it fall over
  - dropping – will the contents break when dropped from a steadily increasing height?

A PRIMARY TEACHER'S HANDBOOK – *Design and Technology* © Folens (not copiable)

𝒫rogression in making structures

Note: This progression is presented as a guide only. It is important to remember that progression is not always linear and that children could be working at many of these stages according to their prior experiences or the learning opportunities presented to them.

Plays and talks about structures made from frameworks, such as climbing frames.

Uses construction kits, push together pieces to make stable structures.

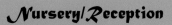

𝒩ursery/𝒭eception

Folds card to make it stand up, eg a picture for display.

Uses found/reclaimed materials to make shelter/home models for animals or story characters.

Identifies and names strong shapes in natural and made structures in the school surroundings.

Makes small 'Jinks' frames for a vehicle chassis.

Uses mouldable foam to make an item to wear, such as a hat for a celebration.

Uses the principles of shell and frame structures when reinforcing model buildings or furniture.

Designs and makes packaging for a product to withstand transport.

Makes a 3D framework using the 'Jinks' technique for a house.

Experiments with construction kits to test strong shapes.

𝒴ear 6

© Folens (not copiable)   A PRIMARY TEACHER'S HANDBOOK – *Design and Technology*

Products and applications

The study of products and applications could be seen as an extension to the activities that already take place in the classroom. For example, classroom displays of stimulus materials have been used to generate discussions for years. Boxes have been disassembled and their nets investigated. Educational toys have been specifically designed for children to take apart and reassemble. However, when investigating, disassembling and evaluating the 'made world' *Design and Technology in the National Curriculum* requires children to develop specific skills.

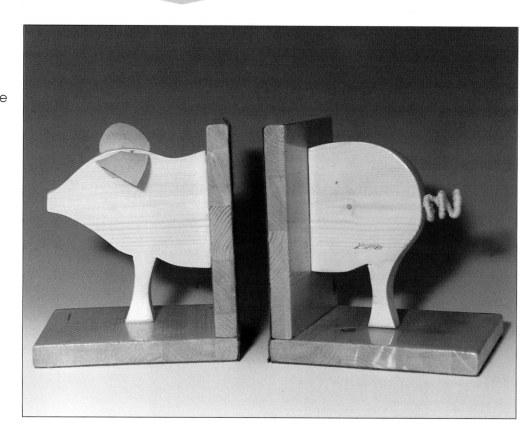

Specific skills

What will the children learn?

By carefully investigating, disassembling and evaluating simple products and applications, the children will learn about the:

- way things work
- various types of materials and components
- use of materials and their fitness for purpose
- principles of how different components are put together
- techniques used to join and reinforce materials.

The children will also develop their understanding of:

- people's needs
- consumer preferences
- texture, the use of colour, quality and specific vocabulary.

Developing products

Although it is unlikely that young children will design new products as a result of their investigations, being able to recognise that existing products were designed for a particular purpose, and that they can be improved, altered and adapted is a vital skill. Professional designers work to meet the perceived needs of consumers in the market place – the extensive range of different types of food products and cars that are available are witness to this.

Products-and-application tasks should be designed to develop these skills. These tasks are often referred to as IDEAs (Investigate, Disassemble and Evaluate Activities) and as children are already discerning consumers of a wide range of products, such as food, clothes, toys and games, carefully structured IDEAs will help to develop their investigative and evaluative skills and increase their critical faculties.

   © Folens (not copiable)

Progression in using products and applications

Investigating and evaluating

A collection of alternative designs for IDEAs provides the children with opportunities to understand what is 'good design'. Readily available products, such as pencil cases, school books, bookends, party hats, bags, clothes, mugs, crisps and sweets, are just a few examples of the range of products that are suitable for investigation in the classroom. Evaluating products is an excellent way of developing the children's critical capability, and it can also provide them with useful ideas for their own designs.

Investigating a whole product

name	what is it?
Oliver	A party hat

this is what it looks like

this is what it should do	this is what it shouldn't do
Fit on your head	Tear when you wear it
does it do this?	does it do this?
yes	sometimes

the most important thing it should do is:
Fit On anyones head

does it do this?
yes it has slots in it

this would make it better: Made from stronger material

Progression

- When asked to talk about familiar products, for example food and toys, children can describe what they like and dislike.
- When describing what products are made from children use the names of different materials.
- By investigating people's likes and dislikes children show their awareness of the needs of others in relation to specific products, for example hats.
- When describing materials from which products are made, children can explain choices that designers have made in terms of simple properties of materials.

- Using a series of structured questions, children can describe a product's fitness for its purpose and make simple suggestions for improvements.
- When investigating and disassembling products, children can identify the function of different parts and describe them using a range of knowledge and understanding acquired from their design and technology experience. They use a vocabulary suitable for their age to describe products.

Questioning

The children should be encouraged to answer structured questions about the products. They should be encouraged to think critically at all times. By approaching product evaluation in this way, they will develop the ability to generate specific design criteria by which they can finally evaluate their own products.

- What is it supposed to do?
- What should a good one do?
- What would a bad one do?
- How well does it do its job?
- How could it be improved?

Disassembling

Taking apart machines, such as an old radio, watch or lock, may be one way of interesting children in the products of technology. However, this will be difficult to resource in the long term. In addition, it may also be out of the context of a design activity because the children would not normally be able to produce a working watch or radio. However, disassembling packaging in order to make a sturdy presentation box for a specific food or gift product can yield exciting developments from the children.

Quality

Defining Quality

Despite having very different personal tastes, most people have an intuitive feel for the quality of a useful object. Defining quality is, however, very difficult. Our view of quality will often be based on how well we feel a product has been made and how well it fits its intended purpose. Quality in the *Design and Technology in the National Curriculum* order now reflects this use of the word.

When a company markets a product, quality is defined in terms of how well a product meets the need of the market for which it is designed. This rejects any arbitrary set of criteria, values or sensitivities.

Quality in designing and making

Children should be taught to consider the following quality issues in their designing and making:

Craft quality
- well made and well assembled
- appropriate precision used in construction
- sympathetic use of materials

Technical quality
- choice of materials justified by reference to properties
- appropriate use of technical systems
- use of scientific knowledge

Fitness for Purpose
- looks good and works well
- meets identified needs
- produced within constraints
- an awareness of energy/material/environmental issues

Progression

Reception/Early years
- Say why they made something.
- Identify who a product is for.
- Describe how they made the product.

KS1
- Find out what people want by asking them.
- Make a simple list of people's needs and preferences.
- Draw a diagram of how a product will be constructed.
- Compare the product with the original design.
- Describe how the design could be changed to make making easier.
- Describe what people think of the product.

KS2
- Find out what people (clients) want by constructing a questionnaire.
- Reflect research in a product specification.
- Write or draw a making schedule.
- Describe changes which occurred in the making process.
- Describe how the design could be changed to make construction more efficient, economical, use less resources and be more environmentally acceptable.
- Evaluate the product with reference to the original clients.

This definition is useful for teachers as they attempt to judge the quality of children's work produced within all the limitations of resources, time and expertise.

As long as children have identified and analysed the need or purpose for their product they can aspire to a quality outcome based on how well the product matches its design intentions.

If they have justifiable criteria for their designing-and-making decisions they should be working towards a quality product.

Vocabulary

It is difficult to teach Technology without using technical names or terms. Names of materials, tools, processes and equipment all require the introduction of an extensive, new and possibly unfamiliar vocabulary. This new language allows the communication of ideas, an important aspect of designing and making. The language of technology offers access to our society – as consumers and makers, children will need to react to the made environment, evaluate its artefacts and suggest improvement.

In introducing this vocabulary, teachers will need to employ all the strategies usually associated with introducing new words. Set out below are some unfamiliar words that the children may encounter.

Materials and components

adhesive	Correx/corriflute
PVA	screw
textile	sandpaper
hessian	dowel
cotton	hardboard
Binca	Plastazote
wool	wire
plastic	

Mechanisms and control

axle	energy	propeller
battery	force	pulley (system)
block and tackle	friction	ratchet
bulb (holder)	gear (train)	resistance
chassis	gearing	reed switch
circuit	hinge	rotary
cog	hydraulics	sensor
conductor	input	shaft
construction kit	lever	short circuit
control	linkage	spacer
crank	load	switch
crocodile clips	mechanism	washer
crown wheel	motor	wheel
current	pivot	winch
effort	pneumatics	worm gear

Processes

blending	Jink's corner
whipping	joint
baking	modelling
dyeing	weaving
batik	knitting
casting	insulation
folding	

Designing

appearance	ingredient	taste test
brainstorming	investigation	ranking
chart	net	technology
components	pattern	template
cross-section	performance	tesselations
customer survey	plan	texture
design brief	prototype	three-
design proposal	questionnaire	dimensional
environment	recipe	transparent
equipment	research	two-
exploded drawing	sketch	dimensional
graphics	system	

Equipment

basin	hole punch
bench-hook	needle
vice	paper drill
bradawl	pliers
circle cutter	safety rule
cutting mat	scales
drill	scissors
file	sieve
glue gun	snips
goggles	surform
grater	whisk
junior hacksaw	

Structures

beam	construction kit
block	framework
compression	load

Safety

Health and safety in the classroom

Working safely in the classroom is everyone's responsibility; teachers, children and other adults in the school.

Just as children are taught to move safely around the school, they will need to become acquainted with safety practice within design and technology. They should be introduced systematically to different types of materials, tools and equipment, and they should be shown how to use tools and resources responsibly.

When undertaking designing-and-making activities, general classroom rules should be adhered to. However, the nature of the designing-and-making activity may require the teacher to remind the children about very specific rules that apply to certain tools and equipment.

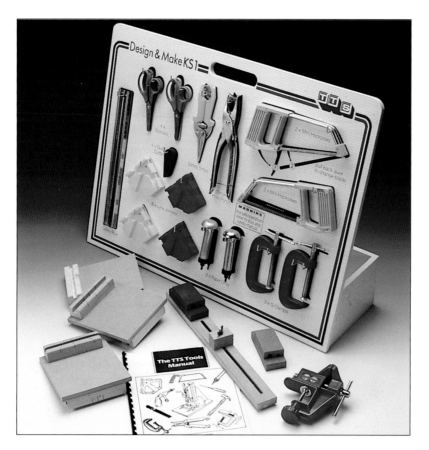

Each time the children use these tools they may have to be reminded of how to handle them properly. However, as the children progress, their ability to remember specific information about tool use should be retained for longer periods and the need to refresh their minds will diminish. It is better to over-emphasise being careful than risk an accident or injury.

Being careful about oneself is of prime importance and children should gradually develop routines that should keep them safe.

Ensuring they are wearing appropriate protective garments, such as aprons or goggles to protect their eyes or masks to protect their face, plays an important role in creating an effective and safe learning environment.

A PRIMARY TEACHER'S HANDBOOK – *Design and Technology* © Folens (not copiable)

Progression in understanding safety

As the children move from class to class, they should find that the rules are consistently upheld by each teacher. Posters designed by older children for younger children can act as useful reminders about how to use tools and equipment safely. They can also demonstrate what protective wear should be worn when working with different materials and also what is the most suitable cover for a particular work surface.

The fear of injuries in the classroom sometimes restricts the types of tools that are made available to the children. The question 'When should specific tools be introduced to the children?' is often asked. The answer is not simple. However, confident teachers, with experience of using tools and equipment correctly, generally introduce children to a wide range of resources.

It is important that teachers develop their children's repertoire of skills in order that they can feel truly confident in a designing and making environment. It may be necessary for INSET to be arranged to meet the needs of individual teachers and schools.

What it says	*What it means*
Key Stage 1	
When acting as consumers and makers the children should: ⚬ consider the hazards and risks in their activities ⚬ follow simple instructions to control risk to themselves.	Children should understand the possible hazards and be taught safe practice in their practical work to minimise risks. When working practically, they follow the instructions and techniques they have been shown. **Example:** Children know that 'germs' carried on their hands can cause sickness and that thorough washing can remove germs. When making a sandwich they wash their hands thoroughly and only touch clean objects while working.
Key Stage 2	
As designers, makers and consumers the children should: ⚬ recognise hazards to themselves and to others in a range of products, activities and environments ⚬ assess risks to themselves and others ⚬ take action to control risks.	Children should be taught the possible hazards and safe practice in their practical work. When working, they should be able to assess risky situations and make sensible decisions on how to reduce the risk, drawing on knowledge they have been taught and techniques they have been shown. **Safety as a consumer** Knowing about food storage and shelf-life of food products. **Safety as a designer** Nuts can be dangerous for young children and some people can be allergic to them. **Safety as a maker** Follow hygienic practices when preparing food products.

Working with Food

Food – a familiar material

Activities related to food have always been popular in primary education. Experiences with food have often focused on its cultural and historical traditions through celebrations. Hygiene and health related aspects are often covered within science and as part of general 'life skills'. The design-and-technology approach to food builds on many of these traditional approaches and also introduces some additional aspects.

A food activity in design and technology is far more than just 'cooking'. The opportunity for children to create a 'real product' without the limitations of materials and the pure fun of working with food are strong incentives to develop this area. They are encouraged to regard food as a material with physical, chemical and organoleptic (taste and textural) properties. When working with food, the properties of food are manipulated according to the nutritional, aesthetic and functional properties required. The context in which food activities are undertaken is therefore important in determining which properties are the focus within a particular design activity.

Opportunities	Typical activities
Changing properties 🖐 Combining and mixing materials to create more useful properties. 🖐 Understanding that the working characteristics of food relate to its use.	🖐 Chocolate has the advantage of its state being changed by gentle heating, and this physical change is reversible when it cools. Children can make small moulded items. 🖐 Syrup can be used to bind together dry ingredients when making flapjacks. 🖐 Flour, sugar and fat go hard when baked into biscuits 🖐 Choose different colours and textures when making a fruit salad. Test alternative combinations using rating tests.
Food in context 🖐 Types of food 🖐 Grouping of food 🖐 Food treatments 🖐 Food availablity	🖐 What is a breakfast? 🖐 Research what people (including themselves) eat for breakfast. Where do the foods come from? What groups of foods are most popular in the survey? How are cereals, eggs, meats and so on produced? How are they processed? 🖐 Design a breakfast that would appeal to most of the guests in a bed and breakfast establishment.
Food and health 🖐 Hygiene 🖐 Storage 🖐 Choice and health	🖐 If you were in charge of the school dinners, could you design a healthy menu for a day or a week? Investigate preferences, costs and the nutritional value of the foods on offer. 🖐 Produce promotional materials to encourage your friends to make healthy choices. 🖐 Make a 'sweet' that is healthy but appealing. Design an exciting new yoghurt and evaluate it using taste tests.

A PRIMARY TEACHER'S HANDBOOK – *Design and Technology* © Folens (not copiable)

𝒫rogression in working with food

Note: This progression is presented as a guide only. It is important to remember that progression is not always linear and that children could be working at many of these stages according to their prior experiences or the learning opportunities presented to them at earlier stages.

Follows a simple recipe to mix a number of dry ingredients represented by symbols.

Investigates people's preferences using a simple taste test.

Produces a simple food product, eg a fruit salad, choosing from a range of ingredients.

Finds out how a group of foods are produced and preserved.

Learns some of the major food groups through preparing an exhibition.

Designs a new food product by adding to an existing product, eg a flavoured yogurt.

Designs and makes a product where the properties of the original ingredients are changed by heating or cooling, eg ice cream.

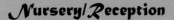

𝒩ursery/𝒫eception

Prepares healthy eating menus for identified client groups, eg infant classes.

𝒴ear 6

© Folens (not copiable)   A PRIMARY TEACHER'S HANDBOOK – *Design and Technology*

Working with textiles

A textile is any fabric, cloth or raw material that is suitable for weaving. In the primary classroom, textiles are generally referred to as material or fabric. Textiles are actually used as construction materials – although this may not be a familiar idea. Items of clothing and accessories, such as hats and bags, are all constructions. They are made from pieces of material, cut, shaped and joined together in a variety of ways to alter the basic properties. Because the properties of textiles differ from each other and from other construction materials, such as wood, card or paper, textiles can be used to create different types of constructions and they can be useful for a variety of purposes. Textiles should not just be associated with aesthetics or decorative effects.

Properties – The microscopic study of weave and the collection, examination and testing of a variety of different textile materials to access the suitability of a range of textiles for a specific task, will help the children to gain knowledge and understanding of properties, including:

- texture
- weight
- strength
- wear-and-tear resistance
- water resistance

Attaching, fixing and securing – A variety of techniques, equipment and tools can be used to fix or secure textile materials temporarily or permanently, such as:

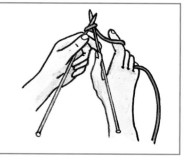

- fabric glue
- Velcro
- rings
- poppers
- hooks and eyes
- pins and pegs
- staples
- buttons
- hand and machine sewing (stitching) – tacking stitches, cross-stitch, running, hemming, blanket, ladder
- frameworks – tucks and gussets, interfacing
- stiffening and reinforcing – stuffing, spraying/treating.

Techniques
- appliqué
- braiding
- crochet
- darning
- embroidery
- knitting
- mesh
- plaiting
- sewing
- spinning
- weaving

Finishing techniques and decorations
- printing – inks, fabric paint
- dying – hot and cold water dyes
- stencils and decorations – fabric crayons and pencils, sequins, buttons
- decorative stitching using different thread

Pattern making
- patterns with straight lines
- patterns with curves
- stencils
- templates

A PRIMARY TEACHER'S HANDBOOK – *Design and Technology* © Folens (not copiable)

Progression in working with textiles

Note: This progression is presented as a guide only. It is important to remember that progression is not always linear and that children could be working at many of these stages according to their prior experiences or the learning opportunities presented to them at earlier stages.

Cuts to shape – simple shapes and patterns.

Nursery/Reception

Makes a 2D collage in which they choose fabric for its properties and join with glue.

Makes a finger puppet or doll, adding other materials as decoration.

Adds colour with crayons.

Disassembles simple textile products, turns into patterns. For example, takes apart a T-shirt to make a paper pattern.

Practises different types of stitches – sewing around shapes they have drawn.

Practises cutting curves.

Makes a product for their own use, eg a pencil case.

Works with easy threads (embroidery) and needles to apply a finish.

Applies finishes using printing inks and appliqué techniques.

Makes a 3D product designed for a client, such as a simple shift for a play.

Year 6

Working with stiff and flexible materials

Working with paper, card and reclaimed materials (impolitely known as 'junk modelling') is now an established part of primary classroom practice. There are limitations to using reclaimed materials and a range of new materials such as corrugated plastic sheet (Corriflute) which is easy to cut and join in a variety of ways have given new possibilities. A range of tools for cutting and scoring and cutting large holes in card, paper and plastic now support more precise work with sheet materials. PVA glue has made for strong fast joints and glue guns have enabled materials such as plastics to be incorporated into products.

Progression in experience

Selects reclaimed materials for their properties, for example transparent flexible, stiff, curved and flat.

Cuts stiff and flexible materials safely, using a variety of tools and techniques as appropriate.

Chooses and cuts materials in an economical way.

Is aware of the economic and environmental issues associated with different materials and the way we use them.

Progression in use

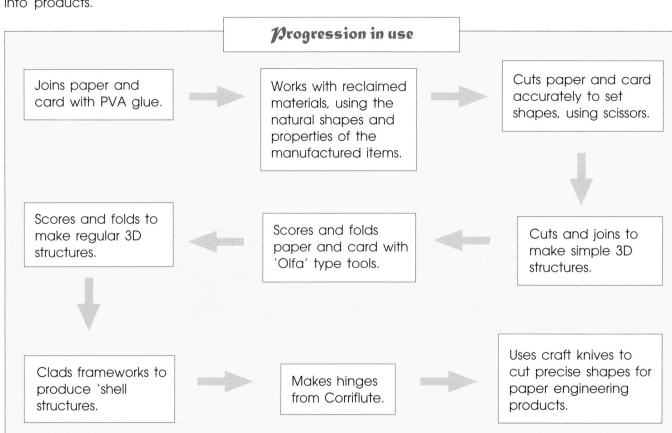

Joins paper and card with PVA glue. → Works with reclaimed materials, using the natural shapes and properties of the manufactured items. → Cuts paper and card accurately to set shapes, using scissors.

Scores and folds to make regular 3D structures. ← Scores and folds paper and card with 'Olfa' type tools. ← Cuts and joins to make simple 3D structures.

Clads frameworks to produce 'shell structures. → Makes hinges from Corriflute. → Uses craft knives to cut precise shapes for paper engineering products.

Working with mechanical and electrical components

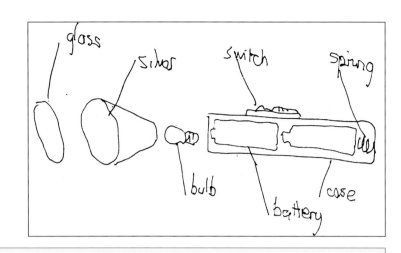

Cross-curricular links

Experience with mechanical and electrical components is closely linked with experiences and knowledge and understanding in the science curriculum. Many of the mechanisms will be met in relation to the use of construction kits but some work will use individual components, such as switches, motors, pneumatics, lights and electromagnets.

Experience	Typical Activities
Key Stage 1	
Construct simple circuits involving batteries, wires, bulbs and buzzers.	Use switches, bulbs, bulb holders and a buzzer to provide lighting and a door bell for a model house built from reclaimed materials.
Make a range of flexible joints using lollipop sticks or stiff cars.	Use lollipop sticks or stiff card to make a puppet with flexible joints. The joints can be made flexible by attaching them together with string or paper fasteners.
Key Stage 2	
Know how switches can be used to control electrical devices. That a complete circuit, including a battery is needed to make electrical devices work. Make a circuit which controls the flow of current. Use pneumatic cylinders to control the movement of a hinge system. Make a range of simple linkages to translate movement in a variety of directions.	Disassemble a torch to investigate how the circuit is made. 

Working with construction kits

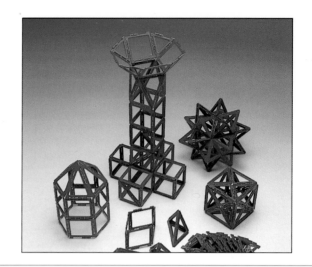

Modelling

Models and modelling have very specific meanings in design and technology. A model is something that represents a simplified version of reality. For example, a LEGO brick can represent part of a wall, a bridge or an animal. Designers use modelling as part of their creative repertoire. Models allow ideas to be developed without making an expensive full scale mock-up. Three-dimensional scale models and computer models allow testing at an early stage of designing, which can avoid expensive mistakes in production.

EXPERIENCE	TYPICAL ACTIVITIES
Children can use models to:	
✋ help with their thinking	Try out ideas, for example a vehicle, with a construction kit before building them from a variety of materials and components.
✋ communicate ideas	Use LEGO Control Lab to show how a fairground ride would work in detail – explain to people how the final idea should work and record their comments.
✋ evaluate a design before building it	Test the stability of a timber-framed house before building it from wood. Alternatively, use boxes, tubes and other reclaimed materials to test for stability before building the framework for a lifting mechanism.
Knowledge and understanding	**Structures** – Bridge kits can be assembled and disassembled to investigate how they can support their own weight as well as loads applied to them. **Mechanisms** – Focused practical tasks and IDEAs can demonstrate how to build gears to change the speed of movement, or pulleys to change the direction of a force. **Control** – Electrical and mechanical components, such as motors and pneumatic cylinders can be used to control the movement in models. Commands may be made via a computer program.
Develop designing and making skills	Tap the power of children's imagination and encourage creativity in designing. Encourage skills in interpreting a set of instructions. Develop hand-eye co-ordination, manual dexterity and general technical capability and confidence.

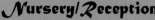

Progression in using construction kits

'Early simple mechanisms' (LEGO) and First Gear introduce the behaviour of mechanical components in an easy-to-construct way.

Nursery/Reception

Free play with push together blocks to build model structures.

Simple gears and cogs, eg First Gear, pushed onto simply made structures.

Structured development of simple vehicles with wheels and axles.

Makes simple linkages to illustrate a range of movements.

Moves from 2D Drawings to 3D models of houses from different structural kits.

Makes simple gears to change the speed and direction of motion.

Investigates computer control modules, eg Fischertechnik and Control Lab, LEGO Technic.

Experiments with models of structures, such as Tudor houses and bridges, to show principles of triangulation with struts and ties.

Makes structures with kits such as TacTic, Teko and Meccano Junior.

Year 6

Uses hand-held battery packs with switches to control motorised models such as vehicles, roundabouts and simple machines.

Working with materials for frameworks

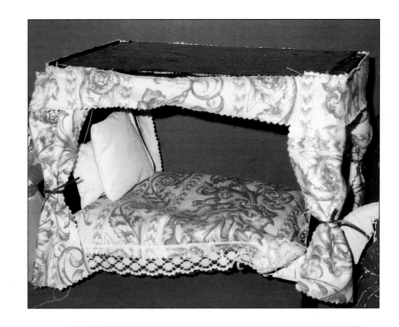

For many teachers, working with more resistant materials, such as wood plastic and metal, presents something of a challenge to their own technological experience. The development of tools and techniques aimed specifically at the primary classroom have had a major impact on what children can achieve when working with resistant materials, such as wood and plastic.

- Techniques for making with wood, such as the 'Jinks' technique, allow even young children to joint wood to make frameworks.
- Jigs for cutting and jointing have improved the quality of joints.
- A variety of ingenious ways of making flexible joints allow mechanisms to be developed.
- A range of affordable components, such as cotton reels, plastic wheels, pulleys and motors are now available to add to children's models.

Manufactured components such as art straws, plastic tubes with connectors and other construction kits are aimed specifically at making framework structures at a higher level of sophistication. Kits also offer the opportunity to investigate basic principles or model ideas prior to making with more expensive consumable materials (see structures section).

Progression in using frameworks

Uses construction kits with structural components and a push together system to build shelters, or containers.

→ Cuts square section wood and dowel using a junior hacksaw and vice. Makes 2D wooden frames, using a 'Jinks' technique.

Uses art straws, joined with pipe cleaners.

← Makes a variety of joints for a class 'display board'.

Uses a bench-hook or jig when cutting wood. → Uses art straws with PVA glue.

Makes more advanced 3D structural models (bridges) from manufactured components, such as a construction kit. ← Makes large structures from rolled paper and tape or canes/dowel and elastic bands.

Makes a 3D framework from wood. Clads frameworks with paper, card or plastic sheet to make them stronger.

Working with mouldable materials

Uses rollers and cutters to form shapes from Plasticine.

Makes a series of set shapes from clay or salt dough.

Designs and makes letters for permanent display from Newclay.

Progression

Nursery/Reception

While mouldable materials are not included in the PoS for Key Stage 1, they are often the starting point for making activities, along with paper, card and reclaimed materials. These materials have strong links with work in art sessions but their use in design and technology will focus on the needs of a client or client group. Children should be introduced to a range of different materials with a variety of properties that make them suitable for different uses. Some of the processes, such as heating or chemical-curing, and the potential chaos which either can create, make them more suitable for work in Key Stage 2.

Experiments with papier mâché.

Moulds a variety of shapes from bread dough before baking.

Experiments with thermoplastic materials, eg Formafoam, Plastizote.

Clay animals produced as gift shop items on sale at the school fête.

Makes a mask for a party with a base made from mouldable foam.

Makes a costume for a school production from a variety of mouldable materials supported by a framework.

Makes house plaques from Plaster of Paris.

Year 6

Makes an item of jewellery from Fymo or Newclay, which is then finished for sale in a school fete.

Differentiating assignments

The principle illustrated here is that almost any type of activity can be differentiated by task. This A-Z collection of ideas gives brief examples of ideas for DMAs, FPTs or IDEAs. Some are based on topic areas, such as V – Victorian Britain, some relate specifically to designing-and-making materials such as C – card and paper, F – food, and others are 'making skills' related. When planning a scheme of work for design and technology, it may be useful to copy the suggested titles on to individually colour-coded index cards – adding further titles as necessary.

All about me
- Use a variety of materials to make:
  - me and my family (decorated cardboard cut-out)
  - my pet (Plasticine creatures)
  - my home (decorated card).

Bags and boxes
- Disassemble bags and boxes.
- Decorate boxes using a variety of materials.
- Design and make different types of containers.

Card and paper
- Cut, shape and join card and paper to make:
  - hat
  - celebration card
  - 3D poster.

Days out
- Use a variety of materials to create a collage showing the:
  - seaside
  - countryside
  - city.

Environments
- Design and make a 'mini' environment in a box to show:
  - beneath the sea
  - under the ground
  - the sky above us.

Food
- Test and taste, cook or bake:
  - taste test for quality in sweet or savoury food products
  - create pocket pitta surprises – anything goes!
  - make balanced 'fancy fillings' for big buns or jacket potatoes.

Games
- Make a game:
  - from reclaimed materials, card and paper
  - about numbers
  - for the playground.

Houses and homes
- Cut, shape and combine card to create a stable farm structure including:
  - farm house
  - barn
  - pig-sty or cow-shed.

In the park
- Design and make:
  - slides
  - roundabouts
  - swings.

Just move it
- Use different materials and equipment to move items using:
  - rollers
  - levers
  - pulleys.

Kits and constructing
- Select a kit to build:
  - a car
  - a structure
  - a moving model.

Life in Tudor Times
- Create a miniature Tudor Village with:
  - houses
  - clay or Plasticine people and animals
  - plants and trees.

Mechanisms and control
- Design and make a:
  - lighthouse
  - well
  - windmill or roundabout.

Night and day
- Use a variety of materials to design and make:
  - night-time creatures;
  - weather scenes
  - weather board.

Open & closed
- Make a model with lids and flaps to show
  - pushing and pulling
  - sliding and tilting
  - swivelling.

Puppets
- Design and make:
  - a paper bag puppet
  - puppet from textiles
  - a puppet from reclaimed materials.

Quick attachments
- Design and make a decorative attachment board showing:
  - hooks and fasteners
  - clips and pegs
  - temporary/permanent attachment techniques.

Reclaimed materials
- Find a way to show different ways of cutting, shaping, joining and finishing:
  - plastic to plastic
  - card and paper to plastic
  - textiles to card, paper and plastic.

Stiff or flexible?
- Use wood and textiles to design and make:
  - a picture frame
  - a deck chair
  - a piece of furniture for a miniature home.

Textiles
- Design and make:
  - a textile collage or wall hanger
  - a woven mat
  - a small decorated bag.

Urban and rural Britain
- Design and make a model of:
  - urban life
  - rural life
  - future urban or rural life.

Victorian Britain
- Design and make a:
  - Victorian street scene model
  - Victorian cardboard stand-up doll
  - piece of Victorian jewellery or item of clothing.

Working wood
- Cut, shape, combine and finish wood to make:
  - a small creature
  - a mobile
  - a container.

Xmas and celebrations
- Use reclaimed materials to design and make:
  - cards
  - table decorations
  - presents and gifts.

Young and old
- Design and make something for a:
  - friend
  - relative
  - manufacturer to produce.

Zips and fasteners
- Design and make:
  - a purse or bag
  - a tying laces teaching toy
  - something with buttons.

Information Technology

The processes involved in designing and making are closely linked with information technology. In industry and commerce children will see computers being used:
- as a basic tool by designers to develop and test ideas
- in manufacturing to control many aspects of the making process.

Children's experience should reflect the use of computers in the wider world. The *National Curriculum for Design and Technology* makes a broad statement about children being 'given opportunity, where appropriate, to develop and apply their information technology (IT) capability'.

Which burger image do you think should be used to illustrate the menu in a fast-food retail outlet?

Opportunities
IT and IDEAs
CD ROM resources can support children's understanding of how technological products work. For example, *The Way things Work* or the *Design File* can provide access to a range of products for children to compare different solutions to the same problem.

IT and focused tasks
Specific skills will need to be taught, such as laying out a block of text in a font of a particular size for inclusion in a greetings card, or controlling a motor through a computer interface.

IT and design and make assignments
There are many ways in which IT can play a part in design and make assignments but sometimes they can be the outcomes of the assignment. For example, children model a lift for a building site with Lego and write a short control routine to control the lift using the input from sensors.

IT and the SEN Code of Practice

The use of IT provides valuable experiences for all children. For those with special educational needs, it is an important tool for providing access to the curriculum, offering alternatives to setting low-level tasks.

IT packages can develop a child's concept of construction at an early stage, providing components for a variety of everyday situations and products, such as cars, bicycles and houses. Later, a 'database' of words and pictures, accessed through an overlay keyboard, can provide a resource to support spelling, vocabulary and illustrations. This enables the children to communicate their ideas.

Children with fine motor skills and manual dexterity problems can use a variety of interface devices to draw and type effectively, and to control models by experimenting with a sequence of commands.

Drawing shapes and lettering on a computer can be far easier than using alternative drawing and writing tools. Producing a variety of designs, in a fraction of the time taken by convential means, allows for discussion about the merits of alternatives and refinements of the outcomes.

Presenting ideas on video or using a tape recorder can give children time to produce a polished presentation.

When designing special educational programmes, IT can provide a valuable alternative route to outcomes expected from the rest of the class. Exploring the potential of IT to produce quality outcomes will provide valuable motivation and pleasure for all children.

Computers in the National Curriculum

Work in Design and Technology that incorporates IT will enable the school to meet the requirements set out in the *National Curriculum for Information Technology*. The National Curriculum identifies two main strands:

- **Handling information**
- **Modelling and control**

As well as forming part of the children's experience, IT tools enable teachers to gather and retain important assessment evidence.

Handling information

- Organise and communicate information about customer preferences through text and graphics, using databases, spreadsheets and desktop publishing.
- Research CD ROMs for information, for example *The Way Things Work*.
- Communicate with designers and manufacturers through electronic mail and Internet links.
- Produce instruction guides and advertising material using a word processing or Desk Top Publishing (DTP) program.
- Video and audio recordings can be used to:
  - explore a design context
  - gather customer preferences and reactions
  - record design ideas
  - communicate the process of designing and making
  - investigate manufacturing processes.
- Use scanned, clip art or drawn images to apply a finish to packaging, fabric or paper.

Modelling

- Try out a variety of different patterns and colourways based on a block print technique using a 'Paint' program.

Controlling

- Build and explore a computer-controlled model production line using a computer control system.
- Illustrate how their control ideas may work in practice, for example Lego Control Lab reports.

Monitoring

- Use sensors and datalogging equipment to investigate design contexts, for example record the temperature of a pet's cage or a miniature greenhouse throughout a 24 hour period. Use the data to suggest how to develop a new environment. Having made the modifications, evaluate the new design against the old one using the same equipment. Use the graphical evidence in a design report.

Cross-curricular links

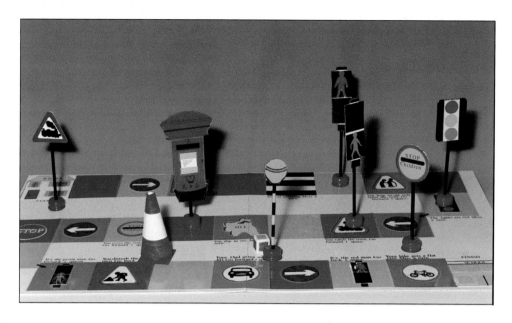

The following examples taken from the PoS for different subject areas shows how design-and-technology activities can be linked across the curriculum. In each of the following, reference is made to designing-and-making skills and the knowledge and understanding that is appropriate to developing design-and-technology capability generally.

English
The pupils should be given opportunities to explore, develop and clarify their ideas, giving reasons for their opinions and actions as well as explaining their choices.

Music
By listening to and appraising sounds, children should be able to develop, communicate and express their ideas and opinions.

Geography
Through thematic study, the children should be able to express views on features of the environment and make recommendations about how the quality could be improved.

Physical Education
The children should be able to talk about what they have done and make simple judgements.

Information Technology
Children should be able to generate and communicate their ideas, using text, tables, pictures and sound.

Mathematics
The children should use purposeful contexts for measuring.

Art
The children should be introduced to the work of artists, craftspeople and designers, including photography, ceramics, textiles, graphic design, architecture, drawing, painting and sculpture.

History
The children should be able to ask and answer questions about the past by using different sources of information, including artefacts, pictures and photographs, and be able to communicate their awareness.

Religious Education
The local agreed syllabus will usually recommend that children are aware of the layout and interior of places of worship. This can be explored through modelling activities.

Science
The children should have knowledge of different types of materials and their uses and they should recognise that materials are used for specific purposes.

Classroom practice and management

The way in which resources for design and technology are made accessible to children is central to the image they will have of the subject. Some schools have equipped a specialised room through which classes rotate, although this can be constraining. Most schools have mobile equipment, suitable for each key stage, which can be located in specific classrooms but moved to others if necessary.

A robust table or workbench, suitable for cutting on, can be equipped with a vice. Tools should be kept secure and yet be made accessible to chidlren when they are working. Large, plastic flip-top toolboxes, or toolboards, are common solutions.

The children need to be able to choose from stock items, such as wood and plastic, and components, such as wheels and axles. Trays and plastic food tubs are very useful if they are kept sorted and labelled.

Organisation of resources

The particular organisation of resources will depend on the confidence of the teacher. Points to consider are:

- preparation of suitable spaces in each room
- schemes – is there a right one for your school?
- books and other stimulus materials
- kits – progression in modelling
- recycled materials
- components – bought materials
- storage of materials
- tools – storage and distribution
- topic boxes.

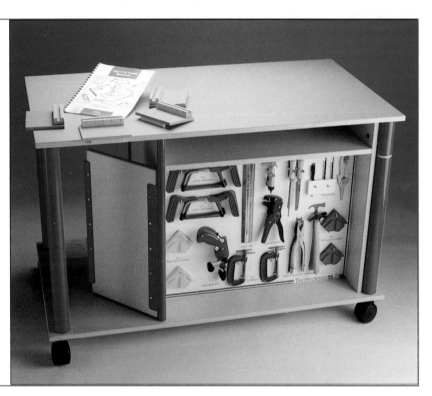

Some useful questions to consider when organising the classroom:

- Where will the tools be stored – toolboard, toolbox, cabinet, underbench cupboard?
- What rules will operate about who can use tools and when?
- How will items be checked back at the end of sessions?
- How will materials be stored?
- How will the children know where materials and components are stored?
- Where and how will the children's work be stored while in progress?
- How will the childrens work be displayed?

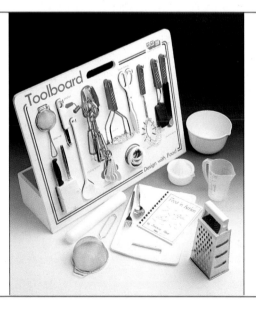

Assessment

Assessment and planning

The purpose of assessment
Teachers assess children to:
- identify and record progress and achievement
- inform the next stage in their learning
- evaluate teaching and learning strategies.

Assessment and planning
Planning a curriculum for children of different abilities requires specific assessment criteria, which should be determined prior to any activity. This involves recognising the exact nature of the learning that will take place. The different sections of this book exemplify the opportunities and experiences which need to be provided to deliver the National Curriculum for design and technology. These also support teachers in interpreting the attainment targets and relating them to specific activities which form part of the programme of study.

Formative assessment
The observations and experiences of working with children on a daily basis provide the most powerful measure of their progress. It is not essential to record the detail of such assessments it will be important to periodically focus on the requirements of the National Curriculum and record impressions to retain some of this informal evidence collected about children's progress.

Summative assessment
For each unit of work it will be necessary to clearly state the leaning objectives and identify opportunities to assess if these have been achieved. Page 11 shows how these would be recorded.

Teaching and Learning Objectives
Writing learning objectives for a unit of work requires a sound understanding of the National Curriculum. Pages 12–14 offer an 'interpretation' of the National Curriculum PoS which could form the basis for writing learning objectives. For example, when making a toy or game the SoW may offer the following objectives:

Learning objectives
- To develop designing skills.
- To be able to communicate their own knowledge of toys and games to describe why they prefer one to another.
- To be able to communicate their ideas for a new toy or game through one or more methods.
- To teach them to evaluate their making in terms of quality.
- To develop knowledge and understanding.
- To use their knowledge of simple mechanisms in their designs.
- To be able to describe how a product would satisfy the needs of the user.
- To be able to describe the properties of the materials they have used when explaining their choices.

Assessment Opportunities
- Listening to the children presenting ideas and evaluation reports.
- Writing or drawings of designs from the 'design file'.
- Observation of 'making' activities.
- Assessment of the final product for the techniques used.

- **To develop making skills.**
  - So that, when making, they can select materials and tools that are appropriate for the task.
  - So that they can use tools safely and effectively.

A PRIMARY TEACHER'S HANDBOOK – *Design and Technology*   © Folens (not copiable)

Assessing progress

Involving children in the assessment process

Assessing designing and making is challenging when children are engaged in practical work. Activity in the room and group work can make individual contributions difficult to record.

One solution is to record though the use of a 'design box'. The children write down, produce annotated sketches, draw or use the teacher to write down their ideas as they progress through an activity. The recorded materials encourage constructive evaluation by the children of their work, and help the teacher to review the attainment levels.

Older children could keep a 'design diary'. These can provide evidence of development and can be useful reminders of previous investigations, disassembly tasks or focused activities.

Making assessment work

If some children need to raise their attainment in a particular area, the teacher will need to add to the planned programme. Some focused tasks could increase knowledge and understanding of an area. For example, in order to develop their experience of mechanisms the class could make a range of flexible joints for display on the classroom wall. For design skills such as planning, an individual problem may be identified. An appropriate response may be to offer some framework upon which the child builds as they plan their design and make assignment, such as the record sheets on page 63.

Opportunities for a range of achievement

Having broad learning objectives means that the children can achieve at a range of levels, if the structure of the task allows them to. When planning the unit of work, judge the range of levels which could be achieved and record this on the planning sheet. Higher levels require more freedom of choice for the children which demands a wider range of teaching and learning strategies to be employed.

	AT1: Designing			AT2: Making		
	Developing Ideas:	**Communicating ideas:**	**Evaluating their designs:**	**Selecting tools and materials:**	**Using tools and processes:**	**Evaluating the product:**
Level 1	handing and assembling materials, components	use pictures and words		select from a narrow range	use given techniques	explain what they are doing
Level 2	draw on experience of materials	use models and pictures	suggest improvements	explain their choices	manipulate tools safely and join materials in a variety of ways	judge their work
Level 3	designs can meet some simple requirements	use labelled sketches	describe ways on which they could develop the design	choose tools and materials purposefully	use tool with some accuracy and precision	the products are similar to original intentions
Level 4	gather views of users	sketches and models show alternative designs	can relate the design to its purpose	can plan making prior to starting	accurately work with a range of materials and techniques	identify what works well and what does not
Level 5	draw on experience of familiar products	use discussion drawing and modelling	can relate the design to its situational use	use a making plan which is modified if necessary	measure and check as the product develops	relate the finished product to their stated intensions
Level 6	use a wide range of sources which could inform the design	models used to explore ideas, use formal drawing	are able to develop design criteria	suggest alternative making strategies if necessary	show precision in making techniques	evaluate products in use and suggest improvements

A PRIMARY TEACHER'S HANDBOOK – *Design and Technology*

Recording and reporting

Recording children's experiences in design and technology is an important addition to recording their achievements.

Recording

Which:

- materials, tools and equipment have been used
- aspects of the design and technology curriculum have been covered, for example food, textiles
- aspects of designing, making and knowledge and understanding have been achieved.

Methods

A number of interesting methods can be used to record pupils experiences that extend beyond conventional checklists and charts.

- **Photographic records** – showing stages of designing and making, as well as the final product.
- **Video tapes** – designed to record a pupil's progress through the stages and also inform other pupils, teachers and parents.
- **Portfolios or files** – a collection of the work produced by individual or groups of children for specific areas such as working with food, wood or textiles.
- **Exhibitions and open events** – to celebrate the children's work and to inform parents and governors.
- **Card indices** – this form of record keeping can easily be transferred, and the types of information they contain can vary according to the colour codes selected.
- **Poster presentations** – a sample collection of work for display around the school.

Recording experience

A good recording system will identify children's progress across the range of opportunities, DMAs, focused tasks and IDEAs. These will be based around one or more of the media areas, such as stiff and flexible materials, constructon kits and so on, identified for the key stage. The knowledge, skills and techniques associated with these materials and components will progress as the child moves through and between the key stages. The necessary flexibility involved in design-and-technology activities makes it easy to allow children to engage in similar activities with different media areas, which can result in a lack of progress between levels. Systematic recording, using criteria related to the progression shown in the level descriptions, can ensure that children are not 'repeating' the same experiences, albeit in a different context.

Record systems

Individual record systems are an effective way of recording experience and achievement, but these can be demanding to maintain and many teachers still rely on an annotated mark book. The difficulty with mark books is that the information they contain is ideosyncratic and difficult to transfer between teachers. Individual portfolios are popular and can be manageable if they concentrate on retaining evidence of recent significant development.

Reporting to parents

The technical descriptors employed in the National Curriculum can often mean little to parents out of the context of the activities undertaken by the children. Writing the level descriptions in 'parent speak' will almost certainly be well received.

Record sheets

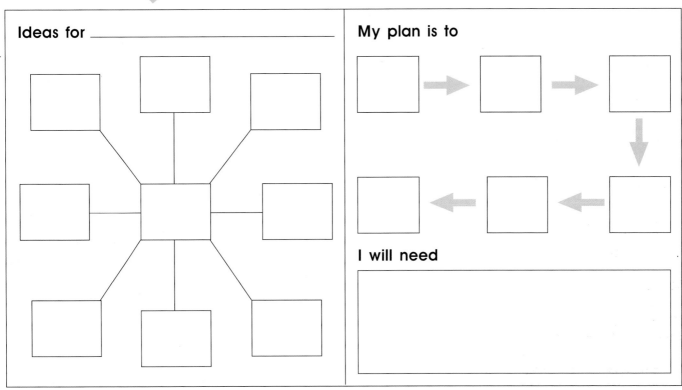

Ideas for _____

My plan is to

I will need

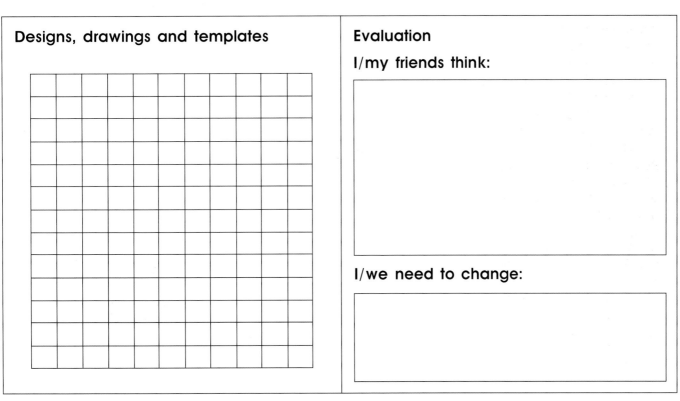

Designs, drawings and templates

Evaluation

I/my friends think:

I/we need to change:

Resources

Additional resources from Folens

Designing and making G Stein (*Key Ideas* series). Ideas for topic-based classroom activities, illustrated in full colour.

The A-Z of Display G Stein (*Key Ideas* series). A collection of ideas for making displays of children's work.

Technology in Action P Harrison, Chris Ryan. A complete design and technology scheme for Key Stages 1 and 2.

Introducing Information Technology and *Developing Information Technology* J & L Lancaster and C Jackson. Two guides for non-specialists on using IT across the curriculum.

NATIONAL BODIES

School Curriculum and Assessment Authority (SCAA)
Newcombe House,
45 Notting Hill Gate,
London W11 3JB.
Tel: 0171 229 1234

Association for Science Education (ASE)
College Lane, Hatfield,
Herts AL10 9AA.
Tel: 01707 267411

Design and Technology Association (DATA)
16 Wellesbourne House,
Walton Road Wellesbourne,
Warwickshire CV35 9JB.
School or individual membership includes journals. An annual conference, local INSET events and publications at reduced rates.

The Design Council
28 Haymarket,
London SW1Y 4SU.
Tel: 0171 839 8000

National Council for Educational Technology (NCET)
Milburn Hill Road, Science Park,
Coventry CV4 7JJ.
Tel: 01203 416994

National Association of Advisors and Inspectors in Design and Technology (NAAIDT)
124, Kidmore Road, Caversham,
Reading, Berks RG4 7NB.

British Nutrition Foundation
High Holborn House,
52–54 High Holborn,
London WC1 6RQ.
Tel: 0171 404-6504

National Dairy Council
5–7 John Princes Street,
London W1M 0AP.
Tel: 0171 499 7822

CLEAPSS School Science Service
Brunel University,
Uxbridge UB8 3PH.
Tel: 01895 251496
Free resources for schools if your LEA is a subscriber.

SUPPLIERS

Technology Teaching Systems Ltd (TTS)
Technology Supplies,
Monk Road, Alfreton.
Tel: 01773 830255
Fax: 01773 830325

Commotion
Unit 11, Tannery Road,
Tonbridge, Kent TN9 1RF.
Tel: 01732 773399

LEGO Dacta (Educational Division) Lego UK Ltd
Ruthin Road, Wrexham,
Clwyd LL13 7TQ.
Tel: 01978 290900

BOOKS AND MATERIALS

General D&T planning
The Good Technology Guide (*DATA and the DfE*)
A comprehensive reference book of resources for design and technology.
Key Stages 1& 2 Design and Technology; the new requirements (*SCAA*)
Tools and Techniques (*CLEAPSS*)
The Big Paper (*Design Council*)
You Can Do It! A technology video for teachers of KS1&2 (*TTS*)

Safety
Be Safe (*ASE*)
Make it Safe (*NAAIDT*)

Piecing Together the NC Jigsaw
Lewisham Professional Development Centre,
Kilmorie Road, London SE23 2SP
Tel: 0181 291 5055

Mechanisms
How Things Work (*Dorling Kindersley*)
Paper Engineering P Gowers and J Salisbury (*Nelson Blackie*)
The Know-How Book of Paper Fun (*Usborne*)
Paper Engineering for Pop-up Books (*Tarquin*)

Control
Primary Robotics (*CLEAPSS*)

Structures
How Things are Built (*Usborne*)

Specific materials
Formafoam Sandi Kendall, Toni Slonecki (*Commotion*)
Working with Plastazote Foam in the Primary Curriculum
Jo Kellaway and Geoff Oliver (*BP Educational Services*)

Construction Kits
Construction Kits L173 from CLEAPSS

Products and Applications
Products and Applications KS1 and KS2 Andrew Loft and Tristram Shepard Impact Education
Tel 01942 748494

Topic Resources
Eyewitness Guides (*Dorling Kindersley*)
Design Technology and Science in a Topic Various titles by Kincaid and Coles (*Hulton*)
Learning from Objects English Heritage ISBN 1 85074 259 6

Information Technology
National Association for Special Educational Needs
4/5 Amber Business Village,
Amber Close, Armington,
Tamworth, Staffs B77 4RP